The Life of Christ

STUDENT BOOK

Purposeful Design Publications is the publishing division of the Association of Christian Schools International (ACSI) and is committed to the ministry of Christian school education, to enable Christian educators and schools worldwide to effectively prepare students for life. As the publisher of textbooks, trade books, and other educational resources within ACSI, Purposeful Design Publications strives to produce biblically sound materials that reflect Christian scholarship and stewardship and that address the identified needs of Christian schools around the world.

Printed in the United States of America
24 23 22 21 20 19 2 3 4 5 6 7

Sky Media, LLC
The life of Christ, student book
ISBN 978-1-58331-273-5 Catalog #MBLCS

Designer: Mike Riester
Editor: John C. Conaway
Illustrations by Ron Adair and Steve Miller
Cover image from Thinkstock.com

Purposeful Design Publications
A Division of ACSI
731 Chapel Hills Dr. • Colorado Springs, CO 80920-3949
Member Care: 800.367.0798 • www.purposefuldesign.com

Contents

Introduction to the Course 4

Getting to Know Who's Who

1: Getting To Know Jesus 8

2: Getting To Know Matthew 12

3: Getting To Know Mark 16

4: Getting To Know Luke 20

5: Getting To Know John 24

Beginnings to Baptism

6: An Angel Brings Good News 30

7: The Savior Is Born! 34

8: Visitors for the Newborn King 38

9: Jesus in the Temple (as a Baby and a Boy) 42

10: The Baptism of Jesus 46

Introducing the Son of God!

11: The Lamb of God! 52

12: Three Temptations 56

13: New Wine Out of Water 60

14: Jesus Tells His Secret to a Lonely Woman 64

15: Jesus Tells His Secret in His Hometown 68

Ministry with His Disciples

16: Four Fishermen Become Fishers of Men 74

17: Faith That Goes Through the Roof 78

18: Jesus' Power over a Storm 82

19: One Boy's Lunch Feeds 5,000 86

20: Jesus Walks on Water 90

Lessons About Life and Death

21: A Glimpse of Glory on a Mountaintop 96

22: Who Will Throw the First Stone? 100

23: Jesus Blesses the Little Children 104

24: Some People Will Do Anything to See Jesus 108

25: A Rich Young Ruler Wants Eternal Life 112

26: Learning About Life and Death—the Hard Way 116

The Road to the Cross

27: Mary Prepares Jesus' Body to Be Buried 122

28: The Plot to Catch and Kill Jesus 126

29: A Grand Entry into Jerusalem 130

30: Disruption at the Temple 134

31: New Meaning to the Passover Meal 138

32: Arrested, Tried and Tortured 142

33: Jesus Goes to the Cross to Die for Us 146

Jesus Is Alive Forever and Ever

34: The Burial and Resurrection 152

35: The Resurrected Jesus Visits Friends and Followers 156

36: Saying Good-Bye and Spreading Good News 160

37: Jesus Selects Another Apostle 164

38: The Devil's Destruction 168

39: God Makes All Things New 172

40: The Teachings of Jesus 176

Introduction to the Course

Who is Jesus?

This may be the most important question you ever ask. Pursuing this question will affect your thoughts, feelings, and actions. It will shape your attitudes, assumptions, morals, and expectations. This course is designed to launch you on the adventure of knowing Jesus.

It's possible that you begin this course with very little knowledge about Jesus. You may have heard people mention Jesus, maybe with very little information; you may have heard positive and negative opinions about him; you may have met people who are embarrassed or offended when the subject comes up. We want to assure you that even if you have very little knowledge about Jesus, this course is designed to equip you with solid information that will help you get to know him well.

It's also possible that you're at the other end of the spectrum. Maybe you've been raised in a Christian family, where you listened to Bible stories, learned to pray, and participated in many conversations about Jesus. Maybe you've gone to church all your life and learned how to study the Bible and how to relate to others in a Christlike way. You may even have spent many years in a Christian school and taken many Bible courses. If that's who you are, what can this course offer you?

No matter where you are on the spectrum, this can be an interesting and helpful course—not just because of what's in the course, but because of what's happening inside of you. At your current stage of life you are going through many changes. One of those changes has to do with your increased ability to think and to understand difficult and complex ideas. As you develop your mental abilities, you will be less and less satisfied with learning a bunch of facts. You'll want to think through what those facts mean in order to understand them and appreciate their importance. So if you know very little about Jesus, you will be learning about him in ways that fit your growing abilities. And if you've been familiar with the facts about Jesus all your life—even if you just took a Jesus course last year—you are changing so fast that you'll understand many of those facts in completely new ways.

In this course, you will be asked to learn many facts about Jesus. But you will also be urged to get to know Jesus himself. Because as you'll see, Jesus is more than a historical person—much more!

How the course works

This course is built around 40 lessons. Your teacher may give you a schedule for reading all the lessons or may specify which ones to read. Each lesson consists of a short account of an event in Jesus' life. Each lesson also contains discussion questions and a short review quiz. The quiz helps you remember specific facts from the story. The discussion questions help you think more deeply about the significance of those facts, how they relate to other facts, and how those truths relate to your life. Sometimes your teacher might have you tear out a page and hand in your answers to the questions.

The lessons are printed in this book; however, you will get more out of a lesson by reading it online at **lifeofchristweb.com**. The online version enables you to look up highlighted words in a glossary and also link you to other features that can help you gain additional information and interact with that information. (Note: The website does not contain the quizzes and discussion questions.)

In addition to working with the lessons in this book, this course will give you the opportunity to do projects that help you gain in-depth knowledge and understanding of subjects that go beyond the lessons. Your teacher will give you instructions and will help you schedule your work. You will also learn to be skillful researchers, whether using online or printed sources. Don't think of these projects as just schoolwork. They give you permission to explore your interests, get answers to your questions, and communicate your findings in creative ways.

The point of it all

If what the Gospels say about Jesus is true, we need to pay attention. He is not only a man but also God. He is our Savior, and he is alive here and now. His teachings are necessary for us today, and he is with us to help us become more and more like him. For over 2,000 years, followers of Christ have learned from him and depended on him and lived for him. He wants us to join all those Christians and become his disciples. And the first step in knowing him is learning about him. That's the purpose of this course. Let's go for it!

Getting to Know Who's Who

Lesson 1: **Getting To Know Jesus**

Topic: Jesus Christ is alive today and wants to be your Savior.

Scripture: John 5:31–47

Key Verse: [Jesus said,] "You diligently study the Scriptures because you think that by them you possess eternal life. These are the Scriptures that testify about me." (John 5:39)

If you read this lesson on **www.lifeofchristweb.com**, be sure to click on the highlighted words and follow the additional links.

Jesus Christ lived about 2,000 years ago. He was never on TV. He never wrote a book. He never traveled very far from where he was born. But Jesus had a greater impact on this world than anyone else who ever lived.

Four books of the Bible tell about the life and teachings of Jesus. These are called the Gospels. *Gospel* means "good news." The good news is that God loves you and has made a way for you to respond to his love and live with him forever. That's the good news Jesus came to bring.

The Gospels were written by four men—Matthew, Mark, Luke, and John; but the Holy Spirit helped these writers say what he wanted them to say. God guided each writer so that what you read in the Bible is God's word. Each writer seemed to have written for a special group of people: Matthew primarily to a Jewish audience; Mark primarily to a Roman audience; Luke to the Gentiles; and John to appeal to every human heart. Each Gospel tells the good news in a slightly different way.

Any history book will tell you what happened a long time ago. The writers of the Gospels had a greater mission. They wrote so people could have a personal relationship with God. John explained, "… these are written that you may believe that Jesus is the Christ, the Son of God, and that by believing you may have life in his name." (John 20:31)

The Gospels are not just made-up stories. Matthew and John were disciples. They saw the events with their own eyes. Mark followed Jesus and wrote what Peter had seen and heard. Luke interviewed people who knew Jesus and carefully checked their stories. Luke wrote, "… it seemed good also to me to write an orderly account for you … so that you may know the certainty of the things you have been taught." (Luke 1:3)

All four Gospels tell us that Jesus lived, died, and rose again. They also tell us that Jesus Christ is alive today and wants to be your Savior.

Discussion Questions **Name** ________________________________

- Why is it important to study the life of Jesus?

- Which books of the Bible give us most of our information about Jesus' life?
  Why are those books called Gospels, and how are they different from other biographies?

- How would you summarize the gospel (or "good news") of Jesus, and why is it good news?

- Why do you think the Holy Spirit inspired four different people to write four different books about the life of Jesus?

- One of the words used to describe Jesus is *Savior*. Why do people need a Savior?

- What questions do you have about Jesus, and why are those questions important to you?

Lesson 1 Review Quiz: Getting To Know Jesus

1. When did Jesus Christ live on earth?

About 2,000 years ago

When dinosaurs roamed the earth

About two million years ago

About two hundred years ago

2. What does the word gospel *mean?*

To whisper the truth

Good news

To run fast

To spell correctly

3. Who wrote the four Gospels in the Bible?

Jesus, Paul, Matthew, and Peter

Matthew, Mark, Luke, and John

Paul, Barnabas, Silas, and Peter

David, Daniel, Luke, and Paul

4. Why were the Gospels written?

So that you may believe that Jesus is the Son of God.

So that you will have life because you belong to him.

So you can have a personal relationship with God.

All of the above.

5. Where did Matthew and John get their information?

They used their imagination and made up stories.

An angel told them.

They saw and heard it with their own eyes and ears.

They interviewed people who were eyewitnesses.

6. Where did Luke get his information?

He interviewed people who had seen and heard Jesus.

He was a follower of Jesus and wrote what he saw.

His mother told him what she saw.

He read it in the Jerusalem newspaper.

Lesson 2: **Getting To Know Matthew**

Topic: God loves everyone—even the worst sinner.

Scripture: Matthew 9:9–10, Matthew 10:1–3

Key Verse: As Jesus went on from there, he saw a man named Matthew sitting at the tax collector's booth. "Follow me," he told him, and Matthew got up and followed him. (Matthew 9:9)

If you read this lesson on **www.lifeofchristweb.com**, be sure to click on the highlighted words and follow the additional links.

As Jesus went on from there, he saw a man named Matthew sitting at the tax collector's booth. "Follow me," he told him, and Matthew got up and followed him. (Matthew 9:9)

Matthew never expected Jesus to call his name! Matthew was a "bad guy." He was a Jew—like Jesus—but he was also a tax collector for the Romans. Jews thought a tax collector was one of the worst kinds of sinners.

Whenever the Romans conquered a country, they forced the people to pay a lot of their money in taxes. If anyone didn't pay his taxes he would be sold into slavery or sent to prison—along with his whole family.

The Romans hired Jews to force other Jews to pay taxes. The Jewish tax collectors didn't just collect what the Romans demanded. They made people pay even more. They kept the extra money for themselves. Matthew worked for the enemy and cheated his fellow Jews. So the Jews hated him. That's why Matthew was surprised when Jesus said, "Come, follow me."

Many of Matthew's friends were viewed as very sinful. He wanted his friends to meet Jesus. So he had a party and invited Jesus. Some people got mad at Jesus for going to a party with these sinful people. But Jesus ignored them. He came to bring sinners back to God. When Jesus chose Matthew, he proved that God loves everyone—even the worst sinner you know.

Matthew changed after he met Jesus. He stopped collecting taxes. As a tax collector, he spread fear and hate. When Matthew became a disciple, he spread good news. What a difference Jesus made in his life!

Matthew came to love the Jews. He knew the Jews wondered: Could Jesus be the promised Messiah? Could he be the promised King of the Jews? Matthew wrote his Gospel to answer their questions.

For the Jews to believe in Jesus, he had to fulfill the prophecies written by Moses and the prophets in the Old Testament. Matthew wanted to prove that Jesus fulfilled prophecy exactly "as it was written." That's why Matthew quotes the Old Testament 65 times.

Discussion Questions Name ______________________________

- What was Matthew's profession before Jesus called him to be a disciple? Why did this make him an unlikely choice to be a disciple?

- What qualified Matthew to write his Gospel?

- What clues do we have that Matthew wrote primarily for a Jewish audience?

- Why do you think Matthew included so many references to the Old Testament?

- What questions do you have about Jesus, and why are those questions important to you?

Lesson 2 Review Quiz: Getting To Know Matthew

1. What was Matthew's job before he met Jesus?

Librarian

Tax collector

Candle maker

Chariot driver

2. What happened to Jews who didn't pay taxes to the Romans?

They had to pay double next year.

They went to bed with no dessert.

They were sold as slaves or sent to prison.

They were crucified.

3. What did Jesus prove by choosing Matthew to be his disciple?

That he liked people whose name starts with the letter "M"

That God loves everyone—even the worst sinner you know

That he didn't know what kind of man Matthew was

That he hated sinners

4. What group of people was Matthew trying to reach?

Other tax collectors

Jews

Romans

Doctors

5. What question was Matthew trying to answer for his audience?

Is Jerusalem the Holy City?

Could Jesus be the promised King of the Jews?

How can a person find Jesus' tomb?

How are Christians supposed to treat each other?

6. Why did Matthew quote the Old Testament so many times?

He had a habit of repeating things.

To prove that Jesus fulfilled Old Testament prophecies.

He couldn't quote the New Testament. It wasn't written yet.

He wanted to show off how well he knew the Bible.

Lesson 3: **Getting To Know Mark**

Topic: Mark, the helper, loved and served Jesus.

Scripture: Acts 13:4–5, 13; Acts 15:36–39

Key Verse: She who is in Babylon … sends you her greetings, and so does my son Mark. (1 Peter 5:13)

If you read this lesson on **www.lifeofchristweb.com**, be sure to click on the highlighted words and follow the additional links.

Mark was a Jewish boy who grew up at an exciting time! He lived in Jerusalem and Jesus came to Mark's house. Sometimes Mark tagged along with the disciples. After Jesus went back to heaven, Mark was part of the first church. Christians had secret prayer meetings at Mark's mother's house.

Mark's cousin, Barnabas, knew the apostle Paul. They planned to sail to faraway lands to spread the gospel. It sounded exciting! Mark wanted to go, so they let Mark join them as their helper. It was exciting!

Early in their mission, Mark decided not to continue on with them. He left Paul and Barnabas and sailed for home. Later, Mark wanted to join them again. Paul said no. He didn't want a helper who might leave them again.

Mark didn't give up doing God's work. He helped Barnabas. Later he helped the apostle Peter. Mark's Gospel is based on what he heard Peter preach. Peter preached mostly to the Romans. So, Mark's Gospel was written to the Romans.

The Romans didn't care about prophecy. All they cared about was who had the most power. So Mark focused on what Jesus did, not what he taught. Mark starts his Gospel when Jesus began his ministry. It covers the last three years of his life. That's when Jesus did miracles, showed his power over nature, healed the sick, brought dead people back to life, died, and rose again. Mark focused on the action and the power.

There's a story in Mark's Gospel not found anywhere else. It happened when Jesus was arrested. Mark wrote, "Then everyone deserted [Jesus] and fled. A young man, wearing nothing but a linen garment, was following Jesus. When they seized him, he fled naked, leaving his garment behind." (Mark 14:50–52) That could have been Mark. Who else would have known? Mark might have been a person who ran away, like he did when he was helping Paul and Barnabas. But even though he may have run away, he never stopped loving and serving Jesus.

Discussion Questions

Name ________________________________

- Why is it important to know that Mark wrote to a Roman audience? How does this fact make his Gospel different from Matthew's?

- How do you think Mark's life experiences helped him become a Gospel writer?

- How can we be confident that what he wrote about Jesus was true?

- What kinds of people do you think would benefit from reading Mark's Gospel?

- What questions do you have about Jesus, and why are those questions important to you?

Lesson 3 Review Quiz: Getting to Know Mark

1. Mark was ...

a Jewish young man who grew up in Jerusalem at the time of Jesus.

a Roman soldier living in Galilee.

not a real person.

one of the wise men who came to see Jesus.

2. Mark based his Gospel stories on ...

what his mother taught him as he was growing up.

something he read in the newspaper.

the sermons he heard the apostle Peter preach.

the teachings of his cousin, Barnabas.

3. Why wouldn't the apostle Paul take Mark along the second time?

He kept talking while Paul was preaching.

He collected taxes for the Romans.

He ran away when they were on a journey to spread the gospel.

He borrowed his best robe without asking.

4. Mark's Gospel was written to ...

Jews.

Romans.

his best friend.

Mark's mother and her Christian friends.

5. Mark's Gospel focused on ...

the teachings of Jesus.

how Jesus fulfilled Old Testament prophecies.

Jesus' actions and his power.

the early years of Jesus' life.

6. What story is found ONLY in Mark's gospel?

Jonah and the great fish

The death of Jesus

A young man running away naked

The birth of Jesus

Lesson 4: **Getting To Know Luke**

Topic: A "reporter's" account of the gospel

Scripture: Luke 1:1–4

Key Verse: Since I myself have carefully investigated everything from the beginning, it seemed good also to me to write an orderly account for you, most excellent Theophilus, so that you may know the certainty of the things you have been taught. (Luke 1:3)

If you read this lesson on **www.lifeofchristweb.com**, be sure to click on the highlighted words and follow the additional links.

Luke was the only Gospel writer who was not Jewish. He was a Gentile, probably from Greece. And he wrote his Gospel primarily to a Greek audience. Luke was a doctor and was highly educated.

Luke was also the only Gospel writer who didn't meet Jesus in person. He became a Christian after Jesus went back to heaven. Then Luke traveled with the apostle Paul to spread the good news about Jesus.

Luke addressed his Gospel to his friend Theophilus, which means "lover of God." Theophilus was a well-respected Gentile and a new believer in Jesus. Theophilus had heard stories about Jesus, but Luke wanted him to be certain his faith was based on the truth. That's why Luke wrote his Gospel.

Luke was like a news reporter. He talked to people who had known Jesus. He was careful to get the story exactly right. His training as a doctor helped him because he knew how important it was to do things without making mistakes. Luke's Gospel includes stories found nowhere else, like the angel's visit to Mary, Jesus' mother, and details about Jesus' birth. He was able to include these stories because he may have talked to Mary personally.

Mark's Gospel was already written. So Luke followed the pattern of Mark's Gospel. But Luke was a Gentile, not a Jew, and he was writing to another Gentile. He wanted to make sure Theophilus knew that Jesus came for everyone. So Luke put in stories that showed how Jesus loved everyone: sick people, women, Samaritans, poor people, shepherds, and beggars.

Luke wrote two books in the New Testament. His Gospel tells about what Jesus BEGAN to do and teach. In the Acts of the Apostles, Luke wrote about what Jesus CONTINUED to do through the church after he went back to heaven. Luke wrote more of the New Testament than any other writer.

Discussion Questions Name ___________________________

- How did Luke's background prepare him to write his Gospel?

- Who was Luke's intended audience?
  Why is it important to remember that fact when reading his Gospel?

- What does Luke tell us about the process he used to write his Gospel?
  How does that affect your confidence in the truth of his writing?

- Why was the book of Acts important as a follow-up to Luke's Gospel?

- What questions do you have about Jesus, and why are those questions important to you?

Lesson 4 Review Quiz: Getting to Know Luke

1. Luke was the only gospel writer who was NOT …

baptized.

Jewish.

a doctor.

left-handed.

2. Luke wrote his Gospel primarily to …

small children.

Hebrews.

a Greek (or Gentile) audience.

King Herod.

3. What was Luke's profession?

Lawyer

Fisherman

Doctor

Gladiator

4. With whom did Luke travel to spread the gospel?

His camel

Apostles Peter and Mark

John, the disciple Jesus loved

Apostle Paul

5. Luke's Gospel is written to Theophilus. His name means …

high and mighty.

lover of animals.

lover of God.

iron man.

6. Luke wrote his Gospel and what other book of the Bible?

1 Corinthians

The Acts of the Apostles

The Revelation of Jesus Christ

2 Luke

Lesson 5: **Getting To Know John**

Topic: John—the disciple Jesus loved

Scripture: John 1–3

Key Verse: But these are written that you may believe that Jesus is the Christ, the Son of God, and that by believing you may have life in his name. (John 20:31)

If you read this lesson on **www.lifeofchristweb.com**, be sure to click on the highlighted words and follow the additional links.

John had been a disciple of John the Baptist. He was one of the first to follow Jesus and became one of Jesus' best friends. In his Gospel, John calls himself "the disciple Jesus loved." John got to sit next to Jesus at the Last Supper, and when Jesus was dying he told John to take care of his mother.

John's Gospel doesn't follow the same pattern as the other three Gospels. Those writers told their stories in the order in which things happened. John doesn't tell his stories in the order they happened. John tells about several miracles or signs Jesus performed. Just like a sign points you in the right direction, the miracles Jesus performed point people to God.

John also tells about several times Jesus said "I am" to describe himself. When God first introduced himself to Moses at the burning bush, Moses asked God his name. God said, "I Am." One time Jesus said to the Jews, "Before Abraham was born, I am!" (John 8:58) Jesus used the same words God used as his name to describe himself. To the Jews, this was the same as saying he was equal with God. So they tried to kill him for saying "I am."

John's Gospel tells about some great conversations Jesus had with people that are not recorded in any of the other gospels. It may be that John was there to overhear what was said. In one of John's letters he said he wrote about what he heard with his ears and had seen with his own eyes.

In one of these conversations, Jesus said what has become the most famous Bible verse: John 3:16! If you know any Bible verse, you probably know that one. It says, "For God so loved the world that he gave his one and only Son, that whoever believes in him shall not perish but have eternal life."

John lived to be very old. He preached about Jesus to the very end. Near the end of his life, he was arrested and sent to a deserted island. There he had a vision of Jesus, of how our world will end, and how Jesus will come back to make all things new. John wrote down his vision as God told him to. It's the last book of the Bible, called The Revelation of Jesus Christ.

Discussion Questions Name ______________________________

- How did John's background prepare him to write his Gospel?

- What was John's purpose in writing his Gospel?
  How well do you think he did in accomplishing this purpose?

- How is John's Gospel different from the other three Gospels?

- Why do you think John 3:16 is quoted so often?

- What questions do you have about Jesus, and why are those questions important to you?

Lesson 5 Review Quiz: Getting to Know John

1. John wrote his Gospel so you may believe that ...

he is a really good writer.

John was the best friend Jesus ever had.

Jesus is the Christ, the Son of God.

the Jewish religion is the best.

2. John said that if you believe Jesus is the Christ, you will ...

have life because you belong to him.

be the smartest kid in your class.

never have any more troubles in life.

have lots of money.

3. What does John call himself in his Gospel?

John, the magnificent

The disciple that sat next to Jesus at the Last Supper

The disciple Jesus loved

John, the brave one

4. While dying on the cross, what did Jesus tell John to do?

Go into all the world and preach the gospel.

Take care of his mother, Mary.

Be sure to obey his parents.

Write down all that he had seen and heard.

5. What did God tell Moses when he asked God's name?

I AM THAT I AM. Tell them I AM has sent you.

My name is God, Almighty, maker of heaven and earth.

My name is Jehovah.

Don't ask again!

6. What book of the Bible did John write while on an island?

1 John

2 John

Island Tales with Old John

The Revelation of Jesus Christ

Beginnings to Baptism
2

Lesson 6: **An Angel Brings Good News**

Topic: God's long-awaited promise is fulfilled.

Scripture: Luke 1:11–22

Key Verse: But the angel said to him, "Do not be afraid, Zechariah; your prayer has been heard. Your wife Elizabeth will bear you a son, and you are to give him the name John." (Luke 1:13)

If you read this lesson on **www.lifeofchristweb.com**, be sure to click on the highlighted words and follow the additional links.

Zechariah served as a priest in God's temple in Jerusalem. Zechariah and his wife, Elizabeth, loved God very much. One thing made the couple sad; they had no children.

The prophets said that God would send a man to prepare the way for the Messiah. Zechariah and Elizabeth would be the parents of this special boy. God sent the angel Gabriel to tell Zechariah the good news.

When it was Zechariah's turn to go into the temple, an angel appeared to him. Zechariah was terrified! The angel told him that Elizabeth would have a son, and that they must name him John. The angel also said, "He will go on before the Lord, in the spirit and power of Elijah—to make ready a people prepared for the Lord." Zechariah couldn't believe it! He doubted the angel, so Gabriel made him unable to speak until John was born.

Six months later, God sent the angel Gabriel to announce another birth. This time he didn't go to a glorious temple. Instead, he went to a small town called Nazareth. He went to see a poor young girl who loved God. Her name was Mary. She was engaged to marry a man named Joseph.

The prophet Isaiah predicted that a virgin would have a baby. He would be called Immanuel, which means "God with us." Mary was the virgin God had chosen. The angel said, "Greetings, you who are highly favored! The Lord is with you." Mary was upset, but the angel calmed her and said, "You will be with child and give birth to a son, and you are to give him the name Jesus. He will be great and will be called the Son of the Most High. The Lord God will give him the throne of his father David, and he will reign over the house of Jacob forever; his kingdom will never end."

Mary had questions, but she did not doubt the angel's message. She welcomed the good news! She told the angel, "I am the Lord's servant … May it be to me as you have said."

Discussion Questions **Name** ____________________

- Why do you think Zechariah had difficulty believing the angel?

- How did Mary respond to Gabriel's announcement?

- What Old Testament passages are referred to in Luke 1?

- How do these passages help us understand Luke 1?

- What questions do you have about Jesus, and why are those questions important to you?

Lesson 6 Review Quiz: An Angel Brings Good News

1. What made Zechariah and Elizabeth sad?

They were getting so old.

Their child was not the Messiah.

They were old and had no children.

They couldn't eat bacon with their eggs.

2. Who came to tell Zechariah good news?

Jesus

The good news delivery service

The angel Gabriel

John the Baptist

3. What did the angel tell Zechariah his child would do?

Prepare a people who are ready for the Lord

Eat grasshoppers and wild honey

Run faster than anyone in all Israel

Make the King very mad

4. What did the angel do to prove himself to Zechariah?

He quoted the prophets perfectly.

He made fire come down from heaven.

He made Zechariah unable to speak.

He flew around the room.

5. Why was the angel Gabriel sent to Nazareth?

To look for a good place for the Messiah to grow up

To amaze the common folks by appearing to them

To deliver food to Mary, who was very hungry

To tell Mary she would give birth to Jesus

6. Gabriel told Mary that Jesus would be called ...

bad names.

the Son of the Most High.

the Salvation of Israel.

the Great One.

Lesson 7: **The Savior Is Born!**

Topic: Looking for a room and a Savior

Scripture: Luke 2:1–20

Key Verse: Today in the town of David a Savior has been born to you; he is Christ the Lord. (Luke 2:11)

If you read this lesson on **www.lifeofchristweb.com**, be sure to click on the highlighted words and follow the additional links.

Mary and Joseph lived in Nazareth. They were newly married and awaiting the birth of the baby growing inside Mary—just as the angel said. When it was almost time for the baby to be born, Caesar Augustus decided to count all the people he ruled. That included the Jews. Mary and Joseph had to go to the town Joseph's family came from—a town called Bethlehem—to be counted there. God had planned their trip ages before. The Messiah was to be born in Bethlehem; that's what the prophets said.

Mary and Joseph traveled by foot and by donkey for many days. When they got to Bethlehem, they must have been tired and hungry. They needed a safe place for Jesus to be born. It was almost time. They looked for a room to rent, but all the rooms were taken. One man took pity on them. He let them sleep in the stable with his animals. That's where Jesus was born. He had no baby clothes, just strips of cloth. He had no crib or blanket, just a feeding trough filled with hay. Jesus had no great earthly welcome, but heaven could not let his birth go unnoticed.

Some poor shepherds were living out in the Bethlehem hills. They were watching their sheep late at night. An angel of the Lord appeared to the shepherds and said, "Do not be afraid. I bring you good news of great joy that will be for all the people. Today in the town of David a Savior has been born to you; he is Christ the Lord. This will be a sign to you: You will find a baby wrapped in cloths and lying in a manger.

"Suddenly a great company of heavenly host appeared with the angels, praising God and saying 'Glory to God in the highest, and on earth peace to men on whom his favor rests.'" Then the angels went back to heaven. And the shepherds hurried to find the Savior.

They found the baby Jesus, and Mary and Joseph, just as the angels said they would. After they had seen the baby, they told everyone what the angels said about this child and what they had seen. The shepherds gave glory to God! Everyone who heard their report was amazed! Mary knew even more than they did. She treasured these things in her heart.

Discussion Questions **Name** ______________________________

- Why did Joseph and Mary travel from Nazareth to Bethlehem?

- Why was it important for Jesus to be born in Bethlehem?

- Why did angels announce Jesus' birth? Why do you think the angels' announcement came to poor shepherds rather than to rich and powerful people?

- What do you think about the people's reaction to the shepherds' message?

- What questions do you have about Jesus, and why are those questions important to you?

Lesson 7 Review Quiz: The Savior Is Born!

1. How did Mary and Joseph both know that Mary's baby was the Messiah?

A talking donkey told them.

They read what the prophets wrote.

They saw his star in the east.

They were both told by an angel.

2. Why did Caesar Augustus force everyone to go to their family's hometown?

He liked to push people around.

He wanted to count all the people he ruled.

He thought they should have a family reunion.

He wanted to help God's will come true.

3. Why was Jesus born in a stable?

Mary and Joseph couldn't afford to rent a room.

All the rooms were taken.

Mary and Joseph liked to camp outside.

Mary and Joseph loved animals.

4. When the angels announced "good news of great joy," who was it for?

All the shepherds

All the Jews

All the local radio stations

All the people

5. What was the good news of great joy that the angels announced?

Today, all your sins are forgiven.

Today, a King has come who will overthrow the Romans.

Today, in the town of David a Savior has been born to you.

Today, you can eat all the candy you want!

6. How would the shepherds know the angels were telling the truth?

A star would be over the place where the baby slept.

A baby would be found wrapped in strips of cloth, lying in a manger.

They would not be able to speak until they found the child.

The angels didn't have any of their fingers crossed.

Lesson 8: **Visitors for the Newborn King**

Topic: Eastern kings come to worship the baby Jesus.

Scripture: Matthew 2:1–12, Numbers 24:17

Key Verse: Magi from the east came to Jerusalem and asked, "Where is the one who has been born king of the Jews? We saw his star in the east and have come to worship him." (Matthew 2:1b–2)

If you read this lesson on **www.lifeofchristweb.com**, be sure to click on the highlighted words and follow the additional links.

God sent Jesus to be a Savior for everyone. God wanted the Jews to know the Savior, so he sent prophets. God wanted other people to know about the Savior too, so he spoke to them in ways they could understand. Far away, to the east of Israel, wise men called Magi were seeking God.

These men studied the stars, trying to find some sign of God or the promised Savior that the Jewish prophets had written about. They had been taught that the promised Messiah would be king of the Jews and a Savior for all people, even the Gentiles.

When Jesus was born in Bethlehem God sent a special star to announce his birth. When the wise men saw the star, they gathered up their finest treasures and set out to find the newborn Savior so that they could worship him. The star led them to Jerusalem. When they got there, they asked where the newborn king of the Jews lived.

Everyone in Jerusalem was upset by their question—and with good reason! The Jews already had a king, King Herod. He would kill anyone he thought might take over his kingdom. He had already killed his wife and some of his children. When the wise men arrived and talked about seeking the NEW king of the Jews, King Herod wanted to destroy him.

King Herod pretended to want to worship the child too. He asked the priests where Scripture said the Messiah would be born. They all agreed: Bethlehem. The prophet Micah made that clear. King Herod invited the wise men to his palace. The King told them to find the child and report back so that he could worship him too. But he really planned to kill him.

The wise men hurried toward Bethlehem with the star leading them all the way. The star stopped over the house where Jesus was staying. When they went inside, they found the child with his mother. They bowed down and worshiped him. They also gave him treasures of gold, frankincense, and myrrh. God had warned them in a dream not to go back to King Herod. So they left the country a different way.

Discussion Questions Name ______________________________

- What do you think was unusual about how God communicated with the Magi?

- What do you think was going through Herod's mind when the Magi reported on their experience? What do you think the priests were thinking?

- What do you think was the significance of the gifts the Magi presented to Jesus?

- What questions do you have about Jesus, and why are those questions important to you?

Lesson 8 Review Quiz: Visitors for the Newborn King

1. How did God tell the Jewish people about the coming Savior?

Moses appeared and told them.

He spoke through the Jewish prophets.

He told the wise men to tell them a Savior was coming.

He spelled Jesus' name in the stars.

2. What did the wise men study?

History

The stars

Ancient civilizations

Ballet

3. The Jewish prophets said the Savior would be ...

a Savior for all people, even the Gentiles.

a Savior only for the Jews.

born in Nazareth.

born in Egypt.

4. What did King Herod want to do when he heard about the newborn king?

Worship the child with the wise men.

Find a way to kill the baby.

Praise God for making his promises come true.

Tell everyone the good news!

5. Which prophet predicted that the Savior would be born in Bethlehem?

Zachariah

Zephaniah

Micah

Samuel

6. What treasures did the wise men bring to baby Jesus?

A painting of the stars

Sheep, oxen, and doves

Gold, frankincense, and myrrh

Three golden crowns, set with rare jewels

Lesson 9: **Jesus in the Temple (as a Baby and a Boy)**

Topic: A very special child

Scripture: Luke 2:21–52

Key Verse: Joseph and Mary took him [Jesus] to Jerusalem to present him to the Lord. (Luke 2:22b)

If you read this lesson on **www.lifeofchristweb.com**, be sure to click on the highlighted words and follow the additional links.

Whenever a Jewish couple had their first son, they took him to the temple to be dedicated to the Lord. They did this in obedience to God's law.

When Mary and Joseph brought the baby Jesus to the temple, an old man named Simeon and an old woman named Anna lived there. Both were very close to God. They prayed to God, and God talked to them by his Holy Spirit.

God promised Simeon that he would see the Messiah with his own eyes. When he saw baby Jesus, he took him in his arms and said, "My eyes have seen your salvation." He also said Jesus would be a light to the Gentiles and bring glory to Israel. Anna came to see Jesus too. She had spent most of her life in the temple, worshipping God, praying, and going without food so she could pray better. Anna was a prophetess. As soon as she saw Jesus, she knew that he was the promised Messiah. She gave thanks to God and told everyone about this special child who would set them free.

Mary and Joseph returned to Nazareth. Every year Jews came together in Jerusalem to celebrate the Passover Feast. Jesus went with his family and a large group from Nazareth every year. When he was twelve, something special happened. After the feast was over, Jesus' parents started on their journey home. They didn't realize it, but Jesus stayed behind in Jerusalem.

Mary and Joseph thought Jesus was somewhere in their group. When they hadn't seen him for a day, they searched among their friends and relatives. But Jesus wasn't there. So they rushed back to Jerusalem to look for him.

Finally after three days, Mary and Joseph found him in the temple. He was sitting with the teachers and priests. He was listening to them and asking questions. The teachers were impressed with how much young Jesus understood. They had no idea that he was the Messiah—the One who was promised in the Scriptures they were discussing! They must have asked Jesus questions too, because they were also impressed with his answers.

Mary and Joseph were upset, as any parent would be. But Jesus said, "Why were you searching for me? Didn't you know I had to be in my Father's house?" They didn't understand what he meant. So Jesus went home with his parents and continued to be obedient to God.

Discussion Questions Name ______________________

- Why was it important for Joseph and Mary to take the baby Jesus to the temple?

- What was significant about the responses of Simeon and Anna?

- Why do you think Luke included the experiences of twelve-year-old Jesus?

- What questions do you have about Jesus, and why are those questions important to you?

Lesson 9 Review Quiz: Jesus in the Temple (as a Baby and a Boy)

1. Why did Jewish parents take their first son to the temple in Jerusalem?

To attend school

To introduce him to all the priests and teachers

To dedicate him to the Lord

For a vacation

2. Name the two people at the temple who knew Jesus was the Messiah.

Anna and Simeon

Luke and Laura

Matthew and Mark

Caiaphas and Herod

3. What feast had Jesus' family just attended when Jesus stayed behind?

The Feast of Tabernacles

The Feast of Trumpets

Thanksgiving Day

The Passover feast

4. Where did Jesus stay in Jerusalem when his parents went home?

The upper room

The Jerusalem Hilton

The temple

The Garden of Gethsemane

5. What was Jesus doing while he was away from his parents?

Fishing at the Jordan River

Preaching the good news of God's kingdom

Sitting with the teachers, listening and asking questions

Doing miracles to impress his friends

6. What did Jesus do when he was found?

He threw a temper tantrum.

He said, "Don't you know I'm the Messiah? I can do what I want!"

He went home with them and was obedient to God.

He hid behind the altar.

Lesson 10: **The Baptism of Jesus**

Topic: Jesus models obedience to the Father.

Scripture: Matthew 3:13–17, Luke 3:21–23, John 1:32–34

Key Verse: Then Jesus came from Galilee to the Jordan to be baptized by John. (Matthew 3:13)

If you read this lesson on **www.lifeofchristweb.com**, be sure to click on the highlighted words and follow the additional links.

The child born to Zechariah and Elizabeth grew up to be the man we know as John the Baptist. He lived and preached in the desert. John was Jesus' cousin. But he didn't know for sure that Jesus was the promised one.

People came from all over Israel to hear John the Baptist. He told people, "Repent, for the kingdom of heaven is near." He told them to change their ways, to turn away from doing wrong, and to turn their hearts toward God. Then he baptized those who responded to his message in the Jordan River.

John the Baptist was very popular with all the people. Religious leaders came from the temple to see what John was doing. John had harsh words for them. He said they were like a nest of poisonous snakes! He made it clear that they too had to change—their hearts and their lives—if God was going to accept them. He said that just being a child of Abraham wasn't enough.

People thought John might be the Messiah. But he told them plainly that he was not. He told the people that one coming after him was greater than he. He was so great, John wasn't worthy to untie his sandal.

God had promised to give John a sign so that he could recognize the Messiah—for sure. The sign was that God would send the Holy Spirit as a dove. And the person on whom the Holy Spirit remained would be the Christ.

When Jesus came to John to get baptized, John recognized his cousin. John wanted Jesus to baptize him, because he knew his own sinful heart. He knew he was in the presence of one who was greater than he. But Jesus said to go ahead and baptize him. It was part of God's plan, so John agreed.

When Jesus was coming up out of the water, the heavens opened and the Holy Spirit came down in the form of a dove. The dove remained on Jesus. Then a voice spoke from heaven, saying, "This is my Son, whom I love; with him I am well pleased." Here we see God, the Father, the Holy Spirit and Jesus, the Son of God, all revealed at once. When John saw and heard this, he knew for sure that Jesus was the Christ.

Discussion Questions

Name ___________________________________

- Why were people getting baptized by John?

- Why did Jesus insist on being baptized?

- Why do we baptize people today?

- What have you been taught about baptism?

- What questions do you have about Jesus, and why are those questions important to you?

Lesson 10 Review Quiz: The Baptism of Jesus

1. Who was the son of Zechariah and Elizabeth?

Herod the Great

Paul the Apostle

Little Zech

John the Baptist

2. What did John the Baptist tell the people who came to him?

You're a nest of poisonous snakes.

You should be a Baptist too.

Repent, the kingdom of heaven is near.

Leave all your possessions and follow me.

3. What did John the Baptist call the religious leaders from the temple?

My esteemed guests

A nest of poisonous snakes

Priests and Levites

Brothers

4. John thought the coming one was so great he didn't feel worthy to ...

stand in his presence.

untie his sandal.

kiss his feet.

eat dinner with him.

5. John the Baptist would know who the Christ was when he saw ...

his name spelled in the clouds.

the Holy Spirit remain on him in the form of a dove.

three pigeons flying around him.

a lightning bolt.

6. What did the voice from heaven say to Jesus?

You are my Son, and I love you. I am very pleased with you.

You must avenge my death!

Go into all the world and preach the gospel.

Repent! The kingdom of heaven is at hand.

3

Introducing the Son of God!

Lesson 11: **The Lamb of God!**

Topic: Jesus, the sacrifice for our sins

Scripture: John 1:15–34

Key Verse: The next day John saw Jesus coming toward him and said, "Look, the Lamb of God, who takes away the sin of the world." (John 1:29)

If you read this lesson on **www.lifeofchristweb.com**, be sure to click on the highlighted words and follow the additional links.

For Jews, a lamb was a familiar symbol. Way back when Moses led the Jews out of Egypt, God told them he was going to send a plague against Egypt. The angel of death would kill the firstborn son in every house. But God provided a way to protect the Jews. Each family was told to kill a lamb and put its blood on the doorposts of their house. If the angel of death saw the blood of the lamb, he would pass over that house and no one there would die. This event was called Passover because God passed over those who sprinkled the blood of the lamb on their doorposts.

Later God said in his law, "When anyone is guilty … he must confess in what way he has sinned and, as a penalty for the sin he has committed, he must bring to the Lord a female lamb or goat from the flock as a sin offering; and the priest shall make atonement for his sin." Every Jew had sinned, and every Jew had sacrificed a lamb to pay for his or her sins. So when John said, "Look, the Lamb of God, who takes away the sin of the world!" they understood. They just didn't know how Jesus would take away their sin.

Then John the Baptist told his disciples, "This is the one I meant when I said, 'A man who comes after me has surpassed me because he was before me.'" This was a strange saying because John was born six months before Jesus. John realized that Jesus had always existed. He lived in heaven—as God—before he came to earth as a baby.

John the Baptist reminded them that Jesus was the one God had pointed out to him. He was the one the Holy Spirit had remained on when it came down from heaven like a dove. John had seen it with his own eyes. He assured his disciples, "I have seen and I testify that this is the Son of God." Before Jesus came, there was a way a Jew could get rid of sin and guilt—that was to kill a lamb and offer its blood to God as a sacrifice. God says all sin must be paid for with death. God sent Jesus to die—to be the sacrifice for everyone's sin. At the first Passover, all those who believed God put lamb's blood on their doorposts. They were protected. Jesus is the Lamb of God. If you want his blood to protect you, you must believe God's promise and ask Jesus to let his death pay for your sins. Then God will pass over your sins and forgive you.

Discussion Questions **Name** ______________________________

- What did the people in Jesus' day think of when they heard the word *lamb*?

- What did John have in mind when he called Jesus "the Lamb of God"?

- Why do you think there were so many animal sacrifices in the Old Testament?

- If a younger student asked you why Jesus died, how would you answer? How can "Lamb of God" help you explain Jesus' crucifixion?

- What questions do you have about Jesus, and why are those questions important to you?

Lesson 11 Review Quiz: The Lamb of God!

1. Who was God going to send to kill the firstborn of Egypt?

A devil

The army of Israel

The Angel of Death

The angel Gabriel

2. What were the Jews told to do so death would pass over their house?

Pray and ask God to protect them.

Go to the temple and sacrifice a lamb or goat.

March around their house seven times.

Put the blood of a lamb on the doorposts.

3. What did God's law say must be done when someone is guilty of sin?

Admit you have sinned and bring a sin offering to God.

Beg God's forgiveness.

Try to be better next time

Do something nice for someone else.

4. What did John the Baptist say about Jesus that was very strange?

When is your birthday?

He existed before I was born.

Is this really the Christ, the Son of God?

Isn't this Joseph's son?

5. How was Jesus the "Lamb of God"?

He wore a woolly coat.

He led a flock of men.

He came to die on the cross as a sacrifice for sin.

He put lamb's blood over the doorposts of his house.

6. How can you apply the sacrifice Jesus made in your life?

Be good from now on.

Believe in Jesus and ask God to let his death pay for your sins.

Put lamb's blood on the door of your house.

Never make a mistake.

Lesson 12: **Three Temptations**

Topic: Resisting the devil and relying on God's Word

Scripture: Matthew 4:1–11

Key Verse: At once the [Holy] Spirit sent him [Jesus] out into the desert, and he was in the desert forty days, being tempted by Satan. He was with the wild animals, and angels attended him. (Mark 1:12–13)

If you read this lesson on **www.lifeofchristweb.com**, be sure to click on the highlighted words and follow the additional links.

Jesus went without eating for forty days and nights. After that he was very hungry. Satan came to him and pointed out stones on the ground. He tried to get Jesus to turn the stones into bread. Jesus said, "It is written: 'Man does not live on bread alone, but on every word that comes from the mouth of God.'" This was a quote from God's Word in the book of Deuteronomy.

Then Satan transported Jesus to the highest point on top of the temple. He tried to get Jesus to jump off and let the angels catch him. The devil quoted a promise from the Bible that said God would make sure the angels caught him. But Jesus knew that wasn't how God wanted him to demonstrate he was God. So Jesus again quoted Deuteronomy, saying, "It is also written, 'Do not put the Lord your God to the test.'"

Finally, the devil took Jesus to a very high mountain. He showed him all the kingdoms of the world in all their glory. Then he said, "All this I will give you, if you will bow down and worship me." Jesus didn't argue with him over who really owned the kingdoms of this world or whether he had the power to offer earthly wealth and glory. He just said, "Away from me, Satan! For it is written: 'Worship the Lord your God, and serve him only.'" Then the devil left him, and angels came to take care of him.

Three times the devil tempted Jesus. And three times Jesus responded by quoting God's Word. The Bible says that everyone will be tempted. Jesus taught us to pray that we would not fall into sin when we are tempted.

Ephesians 6:10–17 teaches that the armor of God can protect us from the devil. Most of the armor is designed to help you resist the devil's evil attacks. There's only one piece of equipment described in that passage that you can use to fight back against the devil. It's the sword of the Holy Spirit—God's Word.

The Word of God is very powerful. The devil could not overcome the Word of God when Jesus used it. You should use it too. The more you memorize and understand the Bible, the better you will be able to fight off temptation.

Discussion Questions   Name ______________________________

- Who is Satan, and why is it important to learn about him?

- What kinds of temptation do you think would be hard for you to resist?

- How did Jesus resist Satan's temptations? What can we learn from his example?

- What questions do you have about Jesus, and why are those questions important to you?

Lesson 12 Review Quiz: Three Temptations

1. Who led Jesus into the wilderness to be tempted?

Satan

A serpent

John the Baptist

The Holy Spirit

2. Jesus went without doing something for 40 days. What was it?

Reading the Bible

Praying

Eating

Throwing stones

3. What did the tempter try to get Jesus to turn the stones into?

A building

An altar

Bread

More stones

4. How did Jesus respond to each temptation?

He argued with Satan.

He did what Satan suggested, then asked forgiveness.

He quoted what his mother had always told him.

He quoted God's Word.

5. What can protect us from the devil's attacks?

Killing an animal

The Armor of God

Eating bread and fish

God's force field

6. What one weapon in the armor of God is for fighting back against the devil?

The sword of the Holy Spirit which is the Word of God

Living water to put out Satan's fires

A spear to pierce evil plans

An ax to cut away all temptation

Lesson 13: **New Wine Out of Water**

Topic: Jesus performs his first of many miracles.

Scripture: John 2:1–11

Key Verse: This, the first of his miraculous signs, Jesus performed at Cana in Galilee. He thus revealed his glory, and his disciples put their faith in him. (John 2:11)

If you read this lesson on **www.lifeofchristweb.com**, be sure to click on the highlighted words and follow the additional links.

Jesus and his mother, Mary, were invited to a wedding in the village of Cana. Mary was already there when Jesus and his disciples arrived. And Mary knew something the other guests didn't know: the host had run out of wine.

In those times it was the custom for wedding celebrations to go on for several days. Guests expected food and wine to be provided every day. It was very embarrassing for the wine to run out. Guests might think the host was rude.

Mary thought Jesus might be able to help. She knew he was the Messiah. Mary said to Jesus, "They have no more wine." She was suggesting that he do something to supply their need. Jesus answered her, "Dear woman, why do you involve me? My time has not yet come."

If Mary was trying to get Jesus to use his power for her purposes, he had to make it clear that his directions came from God the Father. He didn't come to do tricks or show off. He came to do the will of his Father in heaven. Mary didn't try to make Jesus do what she wanted. She told the servants, "Do whatever he tells you." Instead of trying to make Jesus do what she wanted him to do, Mary presented the need to Jesus and trusted him to take care of it in the way he thought best.

Jesus responded to her faith. He saw six large stone water jars. These are the kind the Jews used for special washings to make themselves pure. Each jar could hold up to thirty gallons. Jesus told the servants to fill these jars up to the brim with water, almost a hundred and eighty gallons! That's a lot of water.

The servants obeyed. When the jars were filled with water, Jesus told them to dip some out and take it to the person in charge of the dinner. Imagine how they must have felt. They thought they were dipping plain old water so someone could taste it! When the person in charge tasted it, the plain old water had turned into wonderful new wine.

The person in charge raved about this being the best wine he had ever tasted. He didn't realize how great it really was! The servants did! The disciples did! Mary did! They knew they had seen the glory of God and it brought joy!

Discussion Questions

Name ______________________________

- Why was Jesus at the wedding feast?

- What do you think of the conversation between Jesus and his mother? What questions come to your mind when you read what was said?

- What does this event tell us about Jesus?

- What questions do you have about Jesus, and why are those questions important to you?

Lesson 13 Review Quiz: New Wine Out of Water

1. Jesus and his mother were invited to ...

a funeral for the King.

a birthday party.

a parade.

a wedding.

2. Jesus came to ...

do miracles for his friends.

do the will of his Father in heaven.

see if he could survive a cruel death.

make his mother proud of him.

3. What did Mary tell the servants?

Just wait, I'll talk him into doing what I want.

Jesus always makes the best wine.

Do what Jesus tells you.

Fill the jars to the brim with water.

4. How much water did Jesus turn into new wine?

A whole swimming pool

About one hundred and eighty gallons

Six glasses full

All of the water at the wedding

5. When the person in charge tasted the new wine he said,

This is okay, but I've tasted better.

Who made this?

This is the best wine I've ever tasted.

Jesus is the vine and we are the branches.

6. Who realized this was a miracle and that they had seen the glory of God?

The host and the person in charge of the wedding

All the wedding guests

Mary, the disciples, and the servants

The wine merchant

Lesson 14: **Jesus Tells His Secret to a Lonely Woman**

Topic: Jesus reaches out to despised and forgotten people.

Scripture: John 4:4–42

Key Verse: The woman said, "I know that Messiah" (called Christ) "is coming. When he comes, he will explain everything to us." Then Jesus declared, "I who speak to you am he." (John 4:25–26)

If you read this lesson on **www.lifeofchristweb.com**, be sure to click on the highlighted words and follow the additional links.

The Samaritans were related to the Jews. In times past, the Samaritan Jews married people who were not Jews. They married people who worshiped idols. The Samaritans didn't follow God's rules for worship. After that, the Jews and Samaritans always argued. The Jews hated the Samaritans. They thought God hated the Samaritans too, but Jesus came to offer God's love to everyone.

Samaria is in the middle of Israel. Jesus was coming from Judea. He needed to go to Galilee. Most Jews would walk miles out of their way so they wouldn't have to go through Samaria. They didn't even want to see a Samaritan. Jesus needed to go through Samaria. He wanted to show people that God loves everyone.

Jesus met this woman at Jacob's Well at noon. Most of the women came to the well early in the morning, when it was cool. She waited till noon so she wouldn't meet anyone. She expected them to reject her. You see, she had been married five times. Now she was living with a man who wasn't her husband. Everyone knew that was wrong.

Imagine her surprise when Jesus—a Jewish man—asked her for a drink and spoke kindly to her! She wasn't kind to Jesus. She wanted to argue, but Jesus didn't argue with her. Instead he offered her something she was thirsty for—living water. He offered her eternal life. He offered her God's love and acceptance.

Jesus knew all about her five husbands. He knew about her secret sin, but he didn't look down on her or hate her. He loved her. She had heard that the Messiah would know everything. She wondered if this could be him. And Jesus told her: I who speak to you am he. It was amazing to find the Messiah. It was more amazing that he would speak to her—a rejected sinner.

She ran to tell everyone in town. She wasn't ashamed anymore! She introduced everyone to Jesus. Many of the Samaritans believed in Jesus because of her.

Discussion Questions **Name** ______________________________

- Why did most Jews avoid contact with the people of Samaria?

- What do we know about the Samaritan woman? How would you describe her life?

- Why would most Jews have been shocked at what Jesus did?

- What types of people today are considered outsiders?
  How do you think Jesus wants us to treat those people?

- What questions do you have about Jesus, and why are those questions important to you?

Lesson 14 Review Quiz: Jesus Tells His Secret to a Lonely Woman

1. The woman Jesus met by Jacob's Well was a ...

Democrat.

Publican.

Samaritan.

American.

2. Jews hated Samaritans because they married people who were not ...

from their own country club.

Jewish.

religious.

friendly.

3. Samaria is in ...

the north of Israel.

the middle of Israel.

Egypt.

the south of Israel.

4. What time of day did Jesus meet the woman at the well?

Morning

Night

Evening

Noon

5. What did Jesus offer the woman he met at the well?

Wine he had made from the water

Living water

Bread

Directions to a mountain on which to worship

6. What secret did Jesus know about the woman?

She wore sneakers under her robes.

She was living with a man who wasn't her husband.

She had run away from home.

She had stolen her water jar.

Lesson 15: **Jesus Tells His Secret in His Hometown**

Topic: Jesus is rejected by his friends and neighbors.

Scripture: Luke 4:14–30

Key Verse: He [Jesus] went to Nazareth, where he had been brought up, and on the Sabbath day he went into the synagogue, as was his custom. And he stood up to read. [After reading a prophecy about the Messiah he said to them,] "Today this scripture is fulfilled in your hearing." (Luke 4:16, 21b)

If you read this lesson on **www.lifeofchristweb.com**, be sure to click on the highlighted words and follow the additional links.

Jesus had grown up in Nazareth. He knew everyone and everyone knew him. They had seen him as a boy working with Joseph at the carpentry shop. They knew his mother and his younger brothers and sisters. Jesus had played in their streets. He had gone to their synagogue as a young man. The people of Nazareth heard about the wonders Jesus had been doing and were curious.

Each Sabbath day the Jews came together to hear God's Word. An elder would read from one of the prophets, then encourage them to hope for the Messiah. If a rabbi was visiting, he was invited to read the Scripture and explain it. Jesus was invited to read the Scripture.

He read from the prophet Isaiah. It spoke about how the Messiah would come to preach good news to poor people, to set captives free, to make the blind see again, and announce the year when God would set people free. Jesus stopped reading just before the passage where it promised that God would pay back their enemies. His hometown crowd waited to hear what he would say next. Jesus said, "Today this scripture is fulfilled in your hearing." At first they were amazed and said good things about him. But when they realized that he was implying that he was the Messiah, the crowd turned on him.

People began to say things like, "Hey, wait a minute! Isn't this Joseph's son? We know this guy. Who does he think he is?" Jesus wasn't acting like they expected the Messiah to act. They didn't think of him as the promised one who would bring God's kingdom. They knew him as the carpenter's son.

Jesus told them that prophets aren't accepted in their hometowns. He pointed out stories showing how Elijah and Elisha had to do their miracles for people who weren't even Jews because the Jews had hard hearts. The crowd got mad. How dare Jesus imply that Gentiles were better able to receive the Messiah than they! They got so mad they tried to kill Jesus for being a false prophet.

The mob grabbed him and carried him to the cliff that Nazareth is built on. It's a long drop straight down to the jagged rocks below! Just as they were ready to throw him to his death, he walked through the middle of them and went away. Jesus had a mission to fulfill. He had to preach to people who would believe.

Discussion Questions **Name** ________________________________

- What did Jesus say after reading part of Isaiah 61?

- How were Jesus' words surprising?

- How did the people in Jesus' hometown react to his words?

- Why do you think they responded the way they did?

- What questions do you have about Jesus, and why are those questions important to you?

Lesson 15 Review Quiz: Jesus Tells His Secret in His Hometown

1. In what town did Jesus grow up?

Tarsus

Bethlehem

Cana

Nazareth

2. Where did Jesus usually go on the Sabbath day?

To visit his mother

To church

To the synagogue

To Jerusalem

3. Jesus was invited to read . . .

the Scripture from the prophet Daniel.

the Scripture from the prophet Isaiah.

the latest Nazareth sports scores.

what God the Father told him to write down.

4. What was the first response of the crowd?

They were amazed and said good things about him.

They got angry and wanted to kill him.

They were bored and didn't listen.

They started laughing at Jesus.

5. What question did the crowd ask about Jesus?

Is this truly the Messiah?

Isn't this Mary's son?

Isn't this Joseph's son?

Is he going to be our new rabbi?

6. How did Jesus get away from the angry mob that was trying to kill him?

He fought his way free from them.

He called his disciples to rescue him.

He walked through the middle of them and went away.

A heavenly chariot airlifted him out of their midst.

4

Ministry with His Disciples

Lesson 16: **Four Fishermen Become Fishers of Men**

Topic: Jesus calls and transforms ordinary people to carry out his work.

Scripture: Luke 5:1–11

Key Verse: Then Jesus said to Simon, "Don't be afraid; from now on you will catch men." (Luke 5:10b)

If you read this lesson on **www.lifeofchristweb.com**, be sure to click on the highlighted words and follow the additional links.

Many fishermen lived near the Sea of Galilee, which is really a large lake. Four of these fishermen were Simon Peter, his brother Andrew, James, and his brother John. Each night, they would get into their boats and go out on the lake. They cast large nets into the lake then pulled them in to see what they caught. They kept doing this all night long. Each morning they would come to shore and sell the fresh fish. Then they'd wash their nets and get them ready to use again.

One day Jesus was standing on the shore while the fishermen were washing their nets. Simon Peter and the other fishermen already knew Jesus. They thought he might even be the Messiah, but they were not sure. People crowded in close to hear Jesus teach the word of God. Jesus got into Simon Peter's boat. He asked Simon Peter to push the boat out from the shore a little way.

Jesus sat down in the boat and taught the people. This worked great because Jesus was close enough for everyone to hear and see, but the crowd was kept from pressing in on him. That way, everyone could listen better.

When Jesus finished speaking to the crowd, he told Simon to put the boat out into deep water and cast his nets into the water to catch some fish. Simon and his partners had been fishing all night long. They had cast their nets into the water time and time again. Every time they came up empty. They hadn't caught anything, not even an old sandal! But Peter tried again because Jesus said so.

The nets came up full to overflowing! They caught so many fish that the nets started to break! Simon Peter had to call for help to pull in all the fish. Then there were so many in the boats that both boats started to sink. Simon Peter knew a miracle when he saw one! He knew that Jesus was a holy man of God!

Simon Peter fell down at Jesus' knees and begged Jesus to go away. When people get close to God they realize how sinful they are. That's what happened to Simon Peter. He said, "Go away from me, Lord; I am a sinful man!"

Jesus didn't go away. He called the fishermen into a new line of work. Instead of catching fish and bringing them into a boat, Jesus said they'd catch people and bring them into the kingdom of God. Before this time, they had been interested in Jesus, but now they left everything to follow him to be his disciples.

Discussion Questions   Name ______________________________

- What was it like to be a fisherman on the Sea of Galilee? Share any information you've heard or read.

- Why did Jesus ask to use a fishing boat?

- What does Jesus' miracle tell you about him?

- Why did Simon Peter respond to Jesus the way he did?

- What questions do you have about Jesus, and why are those questions important to you?

Lesson 16 Review Quiz: Four Fishermen Become Fishers of Men

1. What did the fishermen use to try to catch fish?

Spears

Buckets

Nets

Fishing poles

2. What were the names of the four fishermen?

Moses, Elijah, Aaron, and David

Matthew, Mark, Luke, and John

Andrew, Simon Peter, James, and John

Judas, Matthew, Mark, and Jonah

3. When Jesus told Simon to let down his nets for a catch, he said …

No thanks, we've already caught our limit.

I need to take a break. I'm hungry!

I'm getting out of the fishing business.

We've been fishing all night and caught nothing.

4. What happened when Simon Peter obeyed Jesus and let down his nets?

A giant fish came and swallowed them.

Nothing special happened.

They caught so many fish, their nets began to break.

They caught seven crayfish and threw them back.

5. Simon Peter fell down at Jesus' knees and …

washed Jesus' feet.

begged Jesus to let him be a disciple.

begged Jesus to go away because he was a sinner.

began bailing water out of the boat.

6. After this experience, the four fishermen …

began a Bible study called "Fishers of Men."

left everything and followed Jesus.

went home to bed because they were tired.

started cleaning all the fish they caught.

Lesson 17: **Faith That Goes Through the Roof**

Topic: A man is healed with the help of his friends' faith and persistence

Scripture: Mark 2:1–12

Key Verse: Some men came, bringing to him [Jesus] a paralytic, carried by four of them. Since they could not get him to Jesus because of the crowd, they made an opening in the roof above Jesus and, after digging through it, lowered the mat the paralyzed man was lying on. (Mark 2:3–4)

If you read this lesson on **www.lifeofchristweb.com**, be sure to click on the highlighted words and follow the additional links.

When the people of Capernaum heard that Jesus was home, so many of them showed up to hear him that they packed the house. People couldn't even get close to the door. And Jesus taught them God's word.

Four men were determined to get their friend to Jesus. He could not get up or walk at all, so they carried him on a mat. They wanted to ask Jesus to heal him. When they couldn't get through the door, they looked for another way. Most houses in that area had a flat roof that could be used as a patio, with stairs on the side of the house that led up to the roof. The roof was probably made of a thick layer of clay. They dug through the roof and lowered their friend into the presence of Jesus.

Jesus recognized their faith. He told the man, "… your sins are forgiven." Jesus knew the man had two problems: He couldn't walk and he had sins that were not yet forgiven. Jesus had authority to solve both problems. He chose to deal with the sin first. Jesus knew this would upset the teachers of the law.

The teachers of the law spent their whole lives studying God's law, telling people what it meant and how to obey it. They believed that only God could forgive sin. They didn't even expect the Messiah to have that right. When Jesus claimed to be able to forgive sin, he was making himself equal to God. They called this blasphemy. To them, this was the worst sin a person could commit.

Jesus knew what they were thinking. So he said to them, "Why are you thinking these things? Which is easier: to say to the paralytic, 'Your sins are forgiven,' or to say, 'Get up, take your mat and walk'?" This was a hard question. They knew that both forgiveness and healing are impossible without God's help. They also knew that it is easier to SAY someone's sins are forgiven because there would be no way to know whether the sins were forgiven or not. But everyone would be able to see if the man was healed. The teachers couldn't answer Jesus, but he wanted them to know that he has authority to do both. So he told the paralyzed man to get up, take his mat and go home. And he did! Everyone was amazed! They praised God, because they knew that only God could perform such a miracle.

Discussion Questions **Name** ______________________________

- Why do you think Jesus attracted such huge crowds?

- How did the four friends demonstrate their faith?

- Why were the teachers of the law so upset with Jesus?

- How does this event help answer the question, Who is Jesus?

- What questions do you have about Jesus, and why are those questions important to you?

Lesson 17 Review Quiz: Faith That Goes Through the Roof

1. When Jesus came to Capernaum there were so many people that ...

they had to rent a large tent.

people had to climb trees to see Jesus.

they packed the house so much that people couldn't get in the door.

they gave people tickets to come back later.

2. What two problems did the man lowered through the roof have?

He couldn't talk or hear.

He was so sick he couldn't walk, and he was a sinner.

He couldn't get a good seat, and he was blind.

He was afraid of heights, and he was very sick.

3. The roof of the house was probably made of ...

hay.

clay.

marble.

heavy boulders.

4. The teachers of the law spent most of their time ...

studying God's Word, telling people what it meant and how to obey it.

going to the library.

arguing with each other.

bothering Jesus.

5. The teachers of the law were angry with Jesus this time because ...

he healed someone on the Sabbath day.

he did miracles that they couldn't do.

he said he could forgive sins, which only God can do.

he knew the law better than they did.

6. What did Jesus do for the man who couldn't walk?

Healed him so that he could walk.

Gave him money so he could go to a doctor.

Helped him pay for the damage done to the roof.

Gave him pillows so he would be more comfortable on his mat.

Lesson 18: **Jesus' Power over a Storm**

Topic: The extent of Jesus' power and authority

Scripture: Mark 4:35–41

Key Verse: He got up, rebuked the wind and said to the waves, "Quiet! Be still!" Then the wind died down and it was completely calm. (Mark 4:39)

If you read this lesson on **www.lifeofchristweb.com**, be sure to click on the highlighted words and follow the additional links.

Jesus had been busy telling stories called parables to the crowds near the Sea of Galilee. Then he had to explain the meaning of the stories to his disciples. When evening came, Jesus said to his disciples, "Let us go over to the other side [of the lake]." They left the crowds and got into a boat. Other boats came along too.

The Sea of Galilee is a lake that is surrounded by mountains. The air over the lake tends to be hot; the air coming through the mountain passes from the ocean is cool. When the hot air and cool air meet over the lake, WATCH OUT! That mix of hot and cool air creates sudden and violent storms.

Jesus was tired. He went to the back of the boat and fell asleep on a cushion. Suddenly a wild storm arose! How the winds must have howled! Waves even crashed over the sides of the boat. The boat was about to sink! Even though many of Jesus' disciples were used to being on the lake, they were terrified. They knew how dangerous such storms could be.

Jesus' disciples woke him up and said, "Teacher, don't you care if we drown?" Jesus got up and the storm was still raging. Jesus told the storm, "Quiet! Be still!" Immediately the winds died down and the lake became completely calm. The storm obeyed him instantly.

No one had ever seen such a thing. People can't make storms obey them. But Jesus was no ordinary man! The disciples were terrified again. But this time it wasn't the storm that terrified them. It was the power Jesus had over nature. Jesus asked them, "Why are you so afraid? Do you still have no faith?" But no one answered his question.

The disciples asked each other, "Who is this? Even the wind and the waves obey him!" The disciples didn't yet fully understand who Jesus was or the extent of his great power. Jesus' power over the storm demonstrated his authority over creation and the forces of nature. People can't even predict the weather accurately, but Jesus could control it!

Discussion Questions **Name** ___________________________

- Why were the disciples so frightened?

- How did the disciples react to the storm?

- What did Jesus do?
  Why do you think he spoke the way he did?

- How does this event help answer the question, Who is Jesus?

- What questions do you have about Jesus, and why are those questions important to you?

Lesson 18 Review Quiz: Jesus' Power Over a Storm

1. What do we call the stories Jesus told?

Fables

Tall tales

Legends

Parables

2. The mix of hot and cool air over the Sea of Galilee creates ...

lightning.

perfect waterskiing conditions.

sudden and violent storms.

thunder.

3. What happened after Jesus went to sleep on the boat?

The boat sank.

They went back to shore.

Peter tried to walk on water but called for Jesus to save him.

A wild storm arose and waves crashed into the boat.

4. What happened when Jesus woke up?

The disciples told him to hurry to shore.

He asked if everyone knew how to swim.

He told the storm, "Quiet! Be still." And it obeyed!

He told the disciples to row harder.

5. What terrified the disciples after the storm stopped?

That Jesus could read their thoughts.

That the boat started leaking.

That the winds and waves obeyed Jesus' commands.

That Jesus was angry for waking him from his nap.

6. Jesus asked them, "Why are you so afraid? Do you ...

still have no faith?"

know how to swim with your clothes on?"

know that we have a good boat?"

know that we can walk to shore if the boat sinks?"

Lesson 19: **One Boy's Lunch Feeds 5,000**

Topic: God is able to meet our needs

Scripture: John 6:1–14

Key Verse: Jesus then took the loaves, gave thanks, and distributed to those who were seated as much as they wanted. He did the same with the fish. (John 6:11)

If you read this lesson on **www.lifeofchristweb.com**, be sure to click on the highlighted words and follow the additional links.

Jesus' miracles attracted many people. Great crowds of people followed him wherever he went. One day Jesus saw a huge crowd coming toward him. Jesus knew that the people were hungry. He also knew that he was going to feed them. He used this problem as an opportunity to teach his disciples a lesson.

Jesus asked Philip, "Where shall we buy bread for these people to eat?" Philip looked at the massive crowd. He tried to figure out how much they would eat, and how much it would cost to buy that much food. The Bible doesn't say how long it took him to answer, but he figured it out. Philip answered, "Eight months' wages would not buy enough bread for each one to have a bite!"

Andrew pointed out, "Here is a boy with five small barley loaves and two small fish." Perhaps the boy heard Jesus ask about food and offered what little he had. Andrew added, "… but how far will they go among so many?"

Jesus told the disciples to have all the people sit down on the grass. There were about 5,000 men, not counting all the women and children. Then Jesus took the boy's rolls, gave thanks to God and had the disciples start passing the bread out to the hungry people who were seated. He did the same thing with the fish. This was an "all-you-can-eat" lunch. Everyone ate as much as they wanted.

After the people ate, Jesus told his disciples to gather up the scraps so nothing would be wasted. Each of the disciples came back with his basket full of left-over bread and fish; that's twelve baskets full.

The Jews were expecting a prophet like Moses to come. When Moses led the Jews out of Egypt, he fed them in miraculous ways. Jesus' miracle of feeding the 5,000 made the people think he was the prophet they were expecting.

The people were so excited when Jesus fed them that they wanted to force him to be their king. Jesus will be King of Kings one day, but he came to earth the first time to die to pay for our sins. So he left them and went up to a mountain by himself before they tried to make him king.

Discussion Questions Name ___________________________

- Why were the crowds around Jesus so large?

- Compare the words of Philip and Andrew.
  What can we learn about them from their words?
  How can their example be useful for us?

- Why do you think the people linked this miracle with the manna in the wilderness?

- How does this event help answer the question, Who is Jesus?

- What questions do you have about Jesus, and why are those questions important to you?

Lesson 19 Review Quiz: One Boy's Lunch Feeds 5,000

1. Why did large crowds of people follow Jesus?

He did great miracles.

They thought he could make fruit grow on trees.

He promised to free them from the Romans.

He told funny stories all the time.

2. How much money did Philip figure it would take to give everyone a bite?

As much as a person earned in a week

Eight hundred pieces of silver

As much as a person earned in eight months

Thirty pieces of gold

3. What was in the lunch the boy offered to Jesus?

Manna and quail

Five loaves of barley bread and two small fish

One chicken and two fish

A sandwich and an apple

4. How many men did Jesus feed (not counting women and children)?

Five hundred

Fifty thousand

Five thousand

Five

5. How many baskets full of scraps did the disciples collect?

Twelve

One

Five

None

6. What were the people going to try to do to Jesus by force?

Make him their king.

Throw him off a cliff.

Give him a haircut, because his long hair gave him power.

Make him tell them if he was the prophet they expected.

Lesson 20: **Jesus Walks on Water**

Topic: Jesus displays his power and his compassion

Scripture: Matthew 14:22–32

Key Verse: During the fourth watch of the night Jesus went out to them, walking on the lake. (Matthew 14:25)

If you read this lesson on **www.lifeofchristweb.com**, be sure to click on the highlighted words and follow the additional links.

After Jesus fed the 5,000 people, he sent the disciples across the lake on their boat, sent the crowds away, and went up on a mountainside to pray. He was alone there. Jesus stayed on the mountain late into the night. During this time the disciples had traveled a long way from shore. Their boat was going against the wind, and they were being pounded by the waves.

Sometime between three o'clock in the morning and six o'clock in the morning, Jesus decided to go to the other side of the lake. But he did it in a miraculous way. He didn't swim. He didn't take a boat. He walked on top of the water! When the disciples saw him, they were scared! These grown men cried out in fear. They screamed, "It's a ghost! It's a ghost!"

But it wasn't a ghost; it was Jesus. He tried to calm them down. He called out to them, "Take courage! It is I. Don't be afraid." He told them not to be afraid. But that was asking a lot. Can you imagine seeing someone walking on the waves?

Peter wanted to be sure it was really Jesus. He said, "Lord, if it's you, tell me to come to you on the water." Jesus told Peter to come on. Peter actually got out of the boat in the middle of the lake with the wind howling and the waves pounding all around him. And Peter walked on water too. He walked right toward Jesus. Then Peter got distracted by the wind and was afraid again. That is when Peter began to sink.

Peter could still see Jesus standing on top of the water. He called out, "Lord! Save me!" Jesus didn't waste any time. Right away he reached out his hand and caught Peter before he went under. Then Jesus said to him, "You of little faith, why did you doubt?" Maybe Peter doubted because he stopped focusing on Jesus' power and started focusing on his impossible situation.

Then Peter and Jesus climbed into the boat. When they did, the wind died down. Then everyone in the boat worshiped Jesus. They said, "Truly you are the Son of God!"

Discussion Questions

Name ______________________________

- Why were the disciples so frightened?

- What do Peter's words and actions tell us about him?

- Why do you think Jesus walked on the water when he could have taken a boat?

- How does this event help answer the question, Who is Jesus?

- What questions do you have about Jesus, and why are those questions important to you?

Lesson 20 Review Quiz: Jesus Walks on Water

1. Where did Jesus go after he sent the disciples and crowds away?

To a Jerusalem restaurant

Home to pray

To the mountainside to pray

To find new disciples

2. Jesus walked on the water. How did he do this?

He walked very fast.

He walked on rocks.

He rode on two giant fish.

It was a miracle of God.

3. When the disciples saw Jesus, they said, "It's a ghost!" What did Jesus say?

Where have you been?

How many fish do you have?

Start rowing. I'll race you to shore.

Take courage! It is I. Don't be afraid.

4. What did Peter say when he saw Jesus walking on the water?

If it's you, tell me to come to you on the water.

Stay there, we'll throw you a rope.

He is the Christ, the Son of the Living God.

How did you do that?

5. What did Peter say to Jesus when he began to sink?

What did I do wrong?

You lied to me!

Good thing I can swim.

Lord! Save me!

6. What happened when Jesus and Peter climbed into the boat?

The wind died down and the people in the boat worshipped Jesus.

The boat was immediately on shore.

The others jumped out of the boat to see if they could walk on water too.

The boat sank because it was overcrowded.

5 Lessons About Life and Death

Lesson 21: **A Glimpse of Glory on a Mountaintop**

Topic: Jesus gives us a preview of his glory

Scripture: Luke 9:28–36

Key Verse: As he was praying, the appearance of his face changed, and his clothes became as bright as a flash of lightning. Two men, Moses and Elijah, appeared in glorious splendor. . . . (Luke 9:29–30a)

If you read this lesson on **www.lifeofchristweb.com**, be sure to click on the highlighted words and follow the additional links.

Jesus had told his disciples, "Some who are standing here will not taste death before they see the kingdom of God." They didn't realize how soon that would happen. About a week later, Jesus took Peter, James, and John up to a mountaintop to pray. Prayer is very important. Jesus didn't just say a prayer as he went along. He went away from the busyness of life so he could talk at length with his Father in heaven.

Peter, James, and John were sleepy. But something happened that made them wide awake. As Jesus was praying, the appearance of his face changed. He started glowing! His clothes started shining as bright as a flash of lightning. The disciples were getting a glimpse of Jesus in his heavenly glory.

Then two men appeared with Jesus. They were shining in glory too. The disciples recognized these men as Moses and Elijah, two of the most famous men in the Bible. They had lived hundreds of years before. Moses was famous for giving the Jews God's laws and for bringing the Jews out of slavery in Egypt. Elijah was a great prophet who spoke God's word.

They were talking with Jesus about his approaching death and departure from this earth. When Moses led the people out of Egypt, that was called the exodus. Exodus means a departure—to leave one place and go to another. Moses led the Jews out of slavery and toward the land God promised them. Jesus' death on the cross would lead people out of slavery to sin and into the kingdom of God.

When the men started to leave, Peter blurted out, "Master, it is good for us to be here. Let us put up three shelters." Peter wanted to set up little tents for Jesus, Moses, and Elijah. Maybe he thought they would stay longer if he did. Peter didn't really know what he was saying.

Before anyone there could answer Peter, a shining cloud surrounded them and a voice came from the cloud. It was the voice of God the Father. He said, "This is my Son, whom I have chosen; listen to him." Peter didn't make any more suggestions. No one did. They were all flat on their faces before God. When they dared to look up again, Jesus looked normal and he was alone. As they came back down the mountain, Jesus told them not to tell anyone what happened up there—until after he rose from the dead.

Discussion Questions

Name ___________________________________

- Why do you think Jesus took only three disciples to witness his transfiguration?

- Why do you think the disciples responded the way they did?

- What do you think was significant about the fact that Moses and Elijah appeared?

- How does this event help answer the question, Who is Jesus?

- What questions do you have about Jesus, and why are those questions important to you?

Lesson 21 Review Quiz: A Glimpse of Glory on a Mountaintop

1. Who did Jesus take with him to the mountaintop to pray?

Peter, Paul, and Andrew

Mark, Andrew, and Luke

Peter and two angels

Peter, James, and John

2. The men Jesus took with him were sleepy, but what woke them up?

A loud noise

A crash of lightning that struck Jesus.

The smell of bad food

Jesus became as bright as lightning.

3. What two famous people appeared with Jesus?

Moses and David

Moses and Elijah

Moses and Elisha

Adam and Eve

4. When Moses led the people out of Egypt, it was called ...

a miracle

a journey

a genesis

an exodus

5. When Moses and Elijah started to leave, what did Peter say to Jesus?

Let's put up three shelters.

Are you all right?

Who were those two men with you?

You should have seen yourself glow!

6. What did the voice from the cloud say?

Don't tell anyone what you saw until Jesus is risen from the dead.

This is my Son, whom I have chosen; listen to him.

Be still!

One day you too will shine with the glory of God.

Lesson 22: **Who Will Throw the First Stone?**

Topic: No one is righteous but God; no one is able to judge but God

Scripture: John 8:1–11

Key Verse: When they kept on questioning him [Jesus], he straightened up and said to them, "If any one of you is without sin, let him be the first to throw a stone at her." (John 8:7)

If you read this lesson on **www.lifeofchristweb.com**, be sure to click on the highlighted words and follow the additional links.

One morning Jesus came to the temple courtyard. People gathered around and Jesus sat down to teach them. The teachers of the law and the Pharisees interrupted Jesus' teaching session. They brought in a woman who had been caught having sex with a man who was not her husband. This is called adultery.

The Ten Commandments say "Do not commit adultery." The Law of Moses went on to say that people who commit adultery should be put to death. But it said that both people should be punished—not just the woman. If the teachers of the law had really cared about enforcing the law, they wouldn't have let the man get away. They weren't trying to enforce the law. They were trying to trap Jesus.

The teachers of the law said, "In the law Moses commanded us to kill such women by throwing stones at them." This was a tricky trap. The law of Moses did say to execute people who commit adultery, but Jews did not enforce that law under Roman rule. If Jesus said not to kill her, he could be accused of going against Moses. If he said to kill her, he could be accused of going against the Roman government. Either way, he would get in trouble.

They were all waiting for an answer—the people Jesus had been teaching, the woman whose life was in danger, and the teachers of the law. Jesus didn't answer. Instead, he silently bent down and started to write something on the ground with his finger. But they kept asking him. So Jesus stood up and said to them, "If any one of you is without sin, let him be the first to throw a stone at her." Then Jesus bent back down again and wrote on the ground. No one knows what Jesus wrote on the ground. The Bible doesn't say. Maybe he was writing each man's name and the sin he had committed.

Jesus managed to get out of their trap. He agreed that the woman had sinned and even that the sin deserved a death penalty. He just asked them who was perfect enough to condemn her. Not one of them was without sin. Jesus knew this. They did too. One by one, everyone left—from the oldest to the youngest.

Soon only Jesus and the woman were left. Jesus asked her, "Woman, where are they? Has no one condemned you?" She said, "No one, sir." Jesus told her, "Then neither do I condemn you. Go now and leave your life of sin."

Discussion Questions Name ___________________________________

- What sin was the woman guilty of? Why is this a serious sin?

- Why did the religious leaders bring the woman to Jesus?

- How did Jesus respond to the religious leaders?
  Why do you think he responded that way?

- How did Jesus treat the woman?
  What does this event tell us about Jesus?

- What questions do you have about Jesus, and why are those questions important to you?

Lesson 22 Review Quiz: Who Will Throw the First Stone?

1. Why did the teachers of the law and the Pharisees bring a woman to Jesus?

They were trying to trap Jesus.

The woman needed Jesus' help.

The woman was blind and they thought he could heal her.

They thought she was his sister.

2. What did the law say should happen to people who are caught in adultery?

They must be sent to prison.

They must confess in public.

They must be put to death.

They must go home immediately.

3. What did Jesus do in response to the teachers' questions?

He got mad at them.

He picked up a stone to throw at them.

He bent down and wrote something on the ground.

He called lightning from heaven to strike them.

4. What did Jesus write on the ground?

Your words will never hurt me.

No one knows. The Bible does not say what Jesus wrote.

He listed the men's names and their sins.

He spelled out the Ten Commandments.

5. What did Jesus say to the men who questioned him?

You're right. We must follow the law and stone her.

Where is the man she was with? He is guilty too.

Can't we all just get along?

If any one of you is without sin, let him be the first to throw a stone at her.

6. What did Jesus say to the woman after no one found her guilty?

You didn't do anything wrong. Don't worry about it.

Go now and leave your life of sin.

Why did you disobey me?

Go to the temple and offer a sacrifice.

Lesson 23: **Jesus Blesses the Little Children**

Topic: Receiving God's kingdom like a little child

Scripture: Mark 10:13-16

Key Verse: He [Jesus] said to them [the disciples], "Let the little children come to me, and do not hinder them, for the kingdom of God belongs to such as these." (Mark 10:14b)

If you read this lesson on **www.lifeofchristweb.com**, be sure to click on the highlighted words and follow the additional links.

Jesus was teaching in the area of Judea across the Jordan River. His disciples were with him, and crowds of people kept coming to him. Some of the people in the crowd had babies and little children with them. They wanted their children to see Jesus too. Some of the people wanted Jesus to touch their children and lay his hands on them and give them a special blessing.

People in the ancient world believed that blessings worked like magic. If someone laid hands on another person and pronounced a blessing, the blessed person would have God's special favor. It's no wonder that parents wanted Jesus to put his hands on their children and bless them!

The disciples tried to stop people from bringing children to Jesus. They told them to go away. Maybe they thought that the children would bother Jesus. They probably thought they were doing Jesus a favor, but Jesus didn't see it that way. When Jesus saw this, he was angry (Mark 10:14a). He told them to let the little children come to him and not to turn them away. Then Jesus said, "Anyone who will not receive the kingdom of God like a little child will never enter it."

Children had no power. They had no rights. They could not earn money. They were helpless. Everything they received had to be received as a gift. The kingdom of God is like that too. People who think they can earn their way in will never make it. Only people who realize that they have no right to demand entrance to God's kingdom will get in. Salvation is a free gift from God. This is what Jesus meant when he said that we have to receive God's kingdom like a little child.

Jesus welcomed the children. He took them in his arms. He put his hands on them and he blessed them. Can't you just imagine the children laughing and playing all around him? Picture Jesus holding babies and praying for them? Jesus loved the little children, and he used them to teach the grown-ups an important lesson. Parents today still ask Jesus to bless their children.

Discussion Questions **Name** ______________________________

- Why do you think parents were bringing their children to Jesus?

- How do you explain the disciples' attitude toward children?

- How did Jesus treat the children?
  What does this event tell us about Jesus?

- What did Jesus mean when he said people must receive the kingdom of God like a little child?

- What questions do you have about Jesus, and why are those questions important to you?

Lesson 23 Review Quiz: Jesus Blesses the Little Children

1. The people brought their children to Jesus because they wanted him to …

touch them and give them a blessing.

offer them a special place in his kingdom.

make them eat their vegetables.

baptize them.

2. What did the disciples do when they saw people bringing children to Jesus?

Told them to wait in line.

Told them that Jesus was out of blessings.

Tried to stop the children and send them away.

Scolded their parents.

3. What did Jesus say to the disciples about the children?

Whose children are these?

I will help them when they are older.

Let the little children come to me!

Those children are the future of our nation.

4. Salvation is …

a free gift from God.

something you have to work hard to earn.

given to every Jew at birth.

an army you give money to at Christmas.

5. What did Jesus do with the children?

Asked them for one prayer he could answer.

Put his hands on them and blessed them.

Played a harp for them.

Taught them the Ten Commandments.

6. Jesus said we must receive God's kingdom like …

a teacher of the Law of Moses.

a wise old man.

a mighty king.

a little child.

Lesson 24: **Some People Will Do Anything to See Jesus**

Topic: Jesus responds to those who diligently seek him

Scripture: Luke 18:35–19:10

Key Verse: He [the blind man] called out, "Jesus, Son of David, have mercy on me!" (Luke 18:38)
He [Zacchaeus] wanted to see who Jesus was, but being a short man he could not, because of the crowd. (Luke 19:3)

If you read this lesson on **www.lifeofchristweb.com**, be sure to click on the highlighted words and follow the additional links.

Jesus met two men near Jericho who wanted to see him but couldn't. One was a blind man, the other was a short man named Zacchaeus who couldn't see over the crowd. The blind man was sitting by the road begging. In those days disabled people couldn't get regular jobs. They made their living by begging for money along the road where people would go to and from the city.

This blind man heard a commotion and wanted to know what was going on. Someone told him that Jesus was passing by. He had heard about Jesus and believed he was the Messiah. He called out, "Jesus, Son of David, have mercy on me!" "Son of David" is a title for the Messiah, since people expected the Messiah to come from David's family. People told him to be quiet, but he shouted even louder. He wanted to see Jesus! No one was going to stop him!

Jesus stopped and had the man brought to him. Then he asked him, "What do you want me to do for you?" The blind man said, "Lord, I want to see." Jesus said, "Receive your sight, your faith has healed you." Suddenly, he could see! He followed Jesus, praising God, and the people in the crowd joined him.

Jesus and the crowd entered Jericho. A man named Zacchaeus was there. He wanted to see Jesus. He was a chief tax collector, probably the boss of the other tax collectors in that area. That's why he was wealthy. Zacchaeus was very short. He couldn't see over the people, and they wouldn't let him through. He ran ahead of them in time to climb a sycamore-fig tree, so he could see Jesus too.

There he was, perched on a limb, when Jesus stopped and looked up at him. Jesus knew his name. He said, "Zacchaeus, come down immediately. I must stay at your house today." So, he hurried down and welcomed Jesus. The people in the crowd started whispering, "He has gone to be the guest of a 'sinner'." Zacchaeus knew what they meant. As a tax collector, he had become wealthy by stealing from other Jews. Zacchaeus said, "Look, Lord! Here and now I give half of my possessions to the poor, and if I have cheated anyone … I will pay back four times the amount." His heart had changed!

Jesus said, "Today salvation has come to this house." Jesus accepted him as a son of Abraham. He had put his faith in God, just as Abraham had done. Then Jesus told the people, "For the Son of Man came to seek and to save what was lost."

Discussion Questions

Name ________________________________

- Why was the blind man calling out to Jesus?
  What prevented him from getting to Jesus?

- Why did Zacchaeus want to see Jesus?
  What prevented him from getting to Jesus?

- How were Zacchaeus and the blind man different?
  What did they have in common?

- How did Jesus respond to each man?
  What does this lesson tell us about who Jesus is?

- What questions do you have about Jesus, and why are those questions important to you?

Lesson 24 Review Quiz: Some People Will Do Anything to See Jesus

1. Which two men wanted to see Jesus near Jericho?

Zacchaeus and a blind man

Peter and Paul

James and John

Moses and Elijah

2. How did the blind man make his living?

Begging

Fishing

Leading the blind

Singing

3. What did the blind man want Jesus to do for him?

Buy him a house.

Help him get a job.

Give him a seeing-eye dog.

Make him able to see.

4. What did Zacchaeus do for a living?

He was in charge of helping blind beggars.

He was the high priest.

He was the chief tax collector.

He was a camel salesman.

5. What did Zacchaeus do so that he could see Jesus?

He climbed up on a rooftop.

He climbed a sycamore-fig tree.

He climbed an olive tree.

He climbed a hill.

6. Where did Zacchaeus and Jesus go together?

Zacchaeus' tax office

Zacchaeus' boat

The temple to worship God

Zacchaeus' house

Lesson 25: **A Rich Young Ruler Wants Eternal Life**

Topic: Choosing between the kingdom of the world and the kingdom of God

Scripture: Mark 10:17–27

Key Verse: As Jesus started on his way, a man ran up to him and fell on his knees before him. "Good teacher," he asked, "what must I do to inherit eternal life?" (Mark 10:17)

If you read this lesson on **www.lifeofchristweb.com**, be sure to click on the highlighted words and follow the additional links.

Matthew, Mark, and Luke all tell this story. Matthew says the man was young, and Luke calls him a ruler. He was probably some kind of public official. Notice HOW he comes to Jesus. He RUNS up to him. And he FALLS ON HIS KNEES. He has an important question for Jesus. "What must I DO to inherit eternal life?"

He didn't ask how to RECEIVE eternal life. He assumed he had to DO something to EARN it. Jesus taught that living forever with God is a gift to be received, not something people can earn by good deeds. Jesus told the man that no one is good except God. This young man always tried to be good. He thought that being good could get him to heaven. Jesus would teach him; that isn't the way.

Then Jesus said, "You know the commandments." Then he listed God's commands for how we are to treat other people. The man said, "Teacher, all these I have kept since I was a boy." The man really believed this. He probably thought that keeping God's law was just doing the right thing in the way you act. But to truly keep God's commands, a person must obey in his heart, not just his actions. No one can do that perfectly. A person who does not murder may still have hate in his heart. And in God's book, hatred breaks the same law that says, "Do not murder."

Jesus looked at the rich young ruler and loved him. Jesus told him, "One thing you lack. Go sell everything you have and give to the poor, and you will have treasure in heaven. Then come, follow me." When the man heard this, he became very sad. He was rich and wasn't ready to give up his wealth on earth to have riches in heaven. Jesus didn't tell everyone to give away all that they owned. But Jesus knew that this man's wealth kept him from trusting God. In that case he needed to let go of his treasures on earth to get treasures in heaven. And eternal life is worth more than all the money in the world.

The man who had run up to Jesus walked away sad. Jesus told his disciples it is easier for a camel to go through the eye of a needle than for a rich man to enter God's kingdom. A camel is huge. The eye of a needle is the tiny hole that thread goes through. There's no way a camel could go through the eye of a needle! It's impossible! Jesus said it is just as impossible for people to get themselves into God's kingdom. The disciples asked, "Who then can be saved?" Jesus said, "With man this is impossible, but not with God; all things are possible with God."

Discussion Questions   Name ______________________________

- How would you describe the young man in this lesson?
  Think of some positive and negative characteristics.

- What did Jesus think about this young man?

- How did the young man respond to Jesus?
  How do you think the religious leaders would have responded to Jesus' words?

- How would you explain this lesson to someone who doesn't know much about Jesus? How would you connect it with what's going on today?

- What questions do you have about Jesus, and why are those questions important to you?

Lesson 25 Review Quiz: A Rich Young Ruler Wants Eternal Life

1. What did the rich young ruler say when he fell on his knees before Jesus?

I'm not worthy!

The Romans are coming!

You must be the Messiah!

What must I do to inherit eternal life?

2. Jesus told the man, "No one is good except . . .

the Jews."

the ones who believe in me."

Moses."

God."

3. What did the man say after Jesus referred to God's commandments?

Teacher, I have obeyed all those commandments since I was a boy.

I wish I could obey all those, but there are too many.

Those commandments are old-fashioned. No one obeys them anymore.

No one is perfect, except God.

4. How did Jesus feel toward this man when he looked at him?

Jesus was irritated with him.

Jesus was sad.

Jesus looked at him and loved him.

Jesus was angry that he wouldn't follow him.

5. How did the man act when Jesus said to give away his wealth and follow him?

Glad

Mad

Sad

Very bad

6. Jesus said it is easier for a __________ to go through the eye of a needle than for a rich man to enter the kingdom of God.

Rope

Camel

Horse

House

Lesson 26: **Learning About Life and Death—the Hard Way**

Topic: Jesus' power and humanity revealed in the midst of his close friends

Scripture: John 11:1–44

Key Verse: Jesus called in a loud voice, "Lazarus, come out!" The dead man came out, his hands and feet wrapped with strips of linen, and a cloth around his face. (John 11:43b–44)

If you read this lesson on **www.lifeofchristweb.com**, be sure to click on the highlighted words and follow the additional links.

Jesus loved his three friends: Lazarus and his sisters, Mary and Martha. They lived in Bethany about two miles from Jerusalem in Judea. When Lazarus got very sick, Mary and Martha sent for Jesus right away. But Jesus didn't come right away. He purposely waited two whole days. Jesus knew that Lazarus was already dead. He also knew that he would raise him from the dead and give God glory.

The disciples were afraid to go back to Judea. The last time they were there the Jews tried to kill Jesus. But they agreed to follow Jesus, even though they thought they might be killed with him. Jesus told them that Lazarus was asleep and he would go and wake him up. He meant Lazarus was dead; but they didn't understand. So, he told them plainly. "Lazarus is dead, and for your sake I am glad I was not there, so that you may believe. But let us go to him." (John 11:14–15)

When Jesus got to Bethany, the funeral was over. Many people came from Jerusalem to comfort the two sisters. Martha ran to meet Jesus, but Mary stayed home. Martha said, "Lord, if you had been here, my brother would not have died. But I know that even now God will give you whatever you ask."

Jesus told her that Lazarus would rise again. All Jews expected to rise again on the final day of judgment, but that wasn't what Jesus meant. He told Martha, "I am the resurrection and the life. Those who believe in me will live, even if they die. And those who believe in me will never die. Do you believe this?" Martha said, "Yes, Lord! I believe … " Then she went home to get Mary.

Mary ran to meet Jesus and many people followed her. They thought she was going to the tomb. She too said, "Lord, if you had been here, my brother would not have died." She cried and Jesus was deeply moved. When Mary showed Jesus the tomb where the body of her brother lay, Jesus cried too. Some people said, "See how he loved him." Others said, "Could not he who opened the eyes of the blind man have kept this man from dying?"

Jesus told them to take away the stone and open the tomb. Martha reminded him that Lazarus had been dead four days. His dead body would have already started to decay and have a terrible smell. Jesus encouraged her, said a prayer, and called in a loud voice, "Lazarus, come out!" He came out alive but wrapped like a mummy. Then Jesus told them to unwrap him and let him go.

Discussion Questions **Name** ___________________________

- Why did Jesus not go to Bethany as soon as he found out that Lazarus was sick?

- What did Martha and Mary believe about their brother's resurrection?

- Why do you think Jesus cried?

- What does this event tell us about Jesus?

- What questions do you have about Jesus, and why are those questions important to you?

Lesson 26 Review Quiz: Learning About Life and Death—the Hard Way

1. Why did Jesus go to Bethany?

To pay his taxes.

To raise Lazarus from the dead.

To bring flowers to Mary and Martha.

To return books to the library.

2. Why were the disciples afraid to go to Bethany with Jesus?

The last time they were in the area, the Jews tried to kill Jesus.

The people were unfriendly.

There was too much smog.

They thought the Romans would arrest them.

3. What did Jesus find when he arrived in Bethany?

He found his lost treasure.

Mary, Martha, and their friends were mourning the death of Lazarus.

Everyone was happy because Lazarus was well again.

The Jews waiting to kill him.

4. Jesus told Martha, "I am the ______________ and the ______________."

alpha and the omega

Son of Man and the Son of God

resurrection and the life

brightest and the best

5. What did both Martha and Mary say to Jesus?

Is he really dead?

Did you get lost?

Sorry you came all that way. Lazarus is better now.

Lord, I wish you had been here. Then my brother would not have died.

6. What happened when Jesus called out to Lazarus?

Nothing

Lazarus came out of the tomb—alive from the dead.

Lazarus said, "Quiet down! I wasn't really dead."

Everyone else fainted.

6 The Road to the Cross

Ron Adair

Lesson 27: **Mary Prepares Jesus' Body to Be Buried**

Topic: Jesus allows a sacrificial gift to proclaim his coming death and resurrection

Scripture: Matthew 26:6–13

Key Verse: [Jesus said,] "When she poured this perfume on my body, she did it to prepare me for burial." (Matthew 26:12)

If you read this lesson on **www.lifeofchristweb.com**, be sure to click on the highlighted words and follow the additional links.

Jesus told his followers that he had to go to Jerusalem to be arrested and crucified. The disciples didn't seem to fully understand, or maybe they just didn't want to believe it. But one woman, Mary, the sister of Martha and Lazarus, believed Jesus was predicting his own death. She wanted to do something special for Jesus that needed to be done. When someone died, it was the Jewish custom to pour expensive perfume on the body before it was buried. The only time this didn't happen was if the person was put to death for a crime. People who were crucified didn't get a nice funeral. No one had a chance to put perfume on the body of those who were crucified.

Mary believed Jesus when he said he would be crucified. She decided to prepare his body to be buried before he died. She knew she wouldn't have the chance afterward. When Jesus was at the home of a man named Simon, she came to him with a special jar full of very expensive perfume. It cost as much as a person earned in a full year. She broke open the jar and poured every drop on Jesus' head and on his feet. He understood that she was showing her love for him.

When the disciples saw this, some of them got angry. Some of them were harsh with the woman. Judas said, "Why this waste? This perfume could have been sold at a high price and the money given to poor people." She wasn't wasting the perfume. She was giving the best she had to Jesus. But Judas didn't really care about the poor people anyway. He was the disciple who kept the money bags. He was thinking of all the money he could have stolen for himself.

Jesus came to her defense. "Leave her alone," Jesus said. "Why are you bothering this woman? She has done a beautiful thing to me. The poor you will always have with you, but you will not always have me. When she poured this perfume on my body, she did it to prepare me for burial." Then he told them that her act of love and devotion would be told wherever the good news was told, all over the world.

Mary couldn't stop Jesus from being crucified. But she could do something. She did what she could. And Jesus praised her for that. He honored her because she showed her love for him the best way she could.

Discussion Questions

Name ______________________________

- Why did Mary pour expensive perfume on Jesus' head and feet?

- Why do you think some people were against what she did?

- Why did Jesus respond the way he did?

- What does this event tell us about Jesus?

- What questions do you have about Jesus, and why are those questions important to you?

Lesson 27 Review Quiz: Mary Prepares Jesus' Body to Be Buried

1. Jesus told his disciples he had to go to Jerusalem. Why was he going?

To preach.

To take a tour of the old city.

To be arrested and crucified.

To perform miracles for King Herod.

2. Which of the following was the Jewish burial custom at the time of Jesus?

Putting the family pet in the tomb with the person who died

Covering the tomb with gold coins

Gathering at the tomb to sing hymns for seven days

Anointing the body with costly perfumes

3. Why did Mary anoint Jesus with costly perfume?

She had lots of money and didn't like the perfume anyway.

She wanted to see if she could get the disciples angry.

Her friends told her to pour perfume on Jesus.

She was preparing his body to be buried.

4. How much was the perfume worth in money.

A few cents

As much as a person earned in a year

As much as two weeks of your allowance

Five hundred dollars

5. What did Judas do when Mary anointed Jesus?

He tried to put the perfume back in the bottle.

He became angry and said it was a waste.

He stomped out of the room and slammed the door.

He commended her for believing Jesus' prediction of his own death.

6. How did Jesus react to Mary's anointing him?

He said she could have sold the perfume and given the money to poor people.

He was angry.

He said she could take Judas' place as one of his twelve disciples.

He made the disciples leave her alone and said she had done a good thing.

Lesson 28: **The Plot to Catch and Kill Jesus**

Topic: Treachery and betrayal by religious leaders and a trusted friend

Scripture: Matthew 26:1–16

Key Verse: Then the chief priests and the elders of the people assembled in the palace of the high priest, whose name was Caiaphas, and they plotted to arrest Jesus in some sly way and kill him. (Matthew 26:3-4)

If you read this lesson on **www.lifeofchristweb.com**, be sure to click on the highlighted words and follow the additional links.

Some people who had seen Lazarus raised from the dead went back to the chief priests. They told them what Jesus had done. The chief priests and the elders of the people called an emergency meeting. They met at the palace of Caiaphas, the high priest. They were afraid. If Jesus went on performing such powerful miracles, everyone would believe in him. If more Jews believed Jesus was the Messiah, there was more danger from the Romans. The Jewish leaders feared they would lose their positions and the nation. So they made plans to catch and kill Jesus. They planned to kill Lazarus too. When people saw Lazarus alive from the dead, they believed in Jesus!

During their meeting, Caiaphas, the high priest said, "It is better for you that one man die for the people than the whole nation perish." (John 11:50) He didn't say this on his own. He didn't realize that God was speaking through him. He was the high priest. So, God used him to predict that Jesus would die for the people. From then on the Jewish leaders looked for a way to catch and kill Jesus.

As time for the Passover Feast drew near, Jews came to Jerusalem from all over Israel. Everyone was wondering if Jesus would come to the feast. Jesus was staying out of the way until God's proper time. He was the "Lamb of God." He had to die at Passover, not before. The Jewish leaders were on the lookout for Jesus. They wanted to arrest him, but not during the feast. They had to find a sly way to arrest him without people noticing. Many people who were coming to the feast believed in Jesus. They might riot if Jesus was arrested openly.

Several times Jesus told his disciples that he would be handed over to be crucified. Jesus knew he was going to Jerusalem to die! He even knew that one of his own disciples would help in the plot to catch him. Judas Iscariot was the one. Judas went to the chief priests and asked, "What will you give me if I hand Jesus over to you?" So they counted out thirty silver coins for him. From then on Judas looked for a good time to help them catch Jesus. He looked for a time when Jesus would be away from the crowds.

God sent his one and only Son to die to pay for the sin of the whole world. The people planning Jesus' death didn't understand because they didn't believe in him. They just thought they were saving their country. They were able to get Jesus killed, but they didn't save their country. Less than forty years later the Romans destroyed the temple and Jerusalem.

Discussion Questions **Name** ______________________________

- Why were the chief priests and elders against Jesus, and why did they see him as a threat?

- Why do you think the raising of Lazarus (something good) was a problem for the Jewish leaders?

- Why was Jesus going to Jerusalem?

- Why do you think some people are against Jesus today?

- What questions do you have about Jesus, and why are those questions important to you?

Lesson 28 Review Quiz: The Plot to Catch and Kill Jesus

1. Why did the chief priests and elders call an emergency meeting?

The temple was on fire.

A riot had started and the Romans were destroying the city.

They wanted to plan a celebration for Jesus.

They were meeting to decide how to stop Jesus.

2. What did the chief priests plan to do with Lazarus?

Sell tickets for people to see the man alive from the dead.

Ask him what life after death was really like.

Make him die … again.

Question him.

3. What did they decide to do to stop Jesus?

Make him their king.

Arrest him and kill him.

Make him their slave.

Ignore him.

4. What feast were all the Jews coming to celebrate in Jerusalem?

Madrigal Feast

Feast of Temples

Passover

Feast of Trumpets

5. Who agreed to help the chief priests catch Jesus?

Judas Paulus

Judas Iscariot

Bar-Jesus

Barabbas

6. How much did the chief priest pay the disciple who helped them catch Jesus?

Thirty gold coins

Thirty silver coins

Thirty dollars

Nothing

Lesson 29: **A Grand Entry into Jerusalem**

Topic: Jesus is honored as a king

Scripture: Luke 19:28–46

Key Verse: They [the disciples] brought it [a donkey colt] to Jesus, threw their cloaks on the colt and put Jesus on it. As he went along, people spread their cloaks on the road. . . . The whole crowd of disciples began joyfully to praise God in loud voices . . . "Blessed is the king who comes in the name of the Lord!" (Luke 19:35–38)

If you read this lesson on **www.lifeofchristweb.com**, be sure to click on the highlighted words and follow the additional links.

The prophets predicted that the Messiah would make a grand entry into Jerusalem, riding on the colt, a foal of a donkey. Jesus knew the prophecy of Zechariah. It said, "City of Zion, be full of joy! People of Jerusalem, shout! See, your king comes to you. He always does what is right. He has the power to save. He is gentle and riding on a donkey. He is sitting on a donkey's colt."

Jesus approached Jerusalem for the Passover celebration. He sent two of his disciples ahead to get the donkey. He told them to untie it, and if anyone asked why, they were to say, "The Lord needs it." They brought the young donkey to Jesus, threw their coats on its back, and put Jesus on it. They had all been waiting for Jesus to make a public announcement that he was the Messiah. This grand entry into Jerusalem was the sign they were waiting for!

The crowds understood too. Many had seen or heard about his recent miracles: raising Lazarus from the dead and healing the blind man. They praised God for his miracles. They welcomed Jesus as their king, throwing their coats on the ground before him and waving palm branches. Christians today celebrate Jesus' grand entry into Jerusalem on what is called "Palm Sunday."

By the time Jesus came to the place where the road goes down the Mount of Olives the whole crowd was praising God with loud voices. They shouted, "Blessed is he who comes in the name of the Lord!" (This was a prophecy from Psalm 118:26.) They were clearly honoring him as Messiah. There were Pharisees in the crowd. They tried to stop what was happening. They told Jesus, "Teacher, rebuke your disciples!" Jesus replied, "I tell you, if they keep quiet, the stones will cry out." The Messiah king deserved praise and honor!

When Jesus got to where he could see Jerusalem, he began to sob. Oh, how he loved Jerusalem! He said, "I wish you had known today what would bring you peace!" Jesus is the one who brings true peace. But they didn't recognize him, so the truth was hidden from them. Then he prophesied how the city would be surrounded and destroyed. He said, "You didn't recognize the time when God came to you. So your enemies will smash you into the ground. They will destroy you and all the people inside your walls. They will not leave one stone on top of another." This came true when the Romans destroyed Jerusalem in the year A.D. 70.

Discussion Questions Name ______________________________

- Why was it important for Jesus to ride into Jerusalem on a young donkey? Why was that fact significant to the people who saw him?

- How do you explain the reactions of the people of Jerusalem?

- What was significant about Jesus' conversation with the Pharisees?

- Why did Jesus weep over Jerusalem?

- What questions do you have about Jesus, and why are those questions important to you?

Lesson 29 Review Quiz: A Grand Entry into Jerusalem

1. What was Jesus riding when he made his grand entry into Jerusalem ?

The colt of a donkey

A camel

A mighty horse

Nothing—he walked

2. If anyone asked why the disciples untied the donkey, what were they to say?

You don't expect the Messiah to walk into town, do you?

Don't ask questions.

The Lord needs it.

This is my donkey.

3. What do we call the day we celebrate Jesus' grand entry into Jerusalem?

Lent

Good Friday

Palm Sunday

Easter

4. The Pharisees said people should stop praising Jesus. What did Jesus reply?

I tell you, if they keep quiet, the stones will cry out.

I tell you, if they keep quiet, the skies will cry out.

I tell you, if they keep quiet, the trees will cry out.

Stop! Can't you enjoy what you've been waiting for all these years?

5. How did Jesus feel about Jerusalem?

He thought it was a nice place to visit.

He loved Jerusalem and wept for the city.

He liked Nazareth better.

He hated Jerusalem because the leaders rejected him.

6. What mistake did the leaders of Jerusalem make that led to its destruction?

They didn't recognize the time when God came to them.

They trusted in the power of their army, not the power of God.

They removed their walls so enemies could come in.

They followed the traditions of their neighbors.

Lesson 30: **Disruption at the Temple**

Topic: Jesus graphically reminds us of his holiness

Scripture: Matthew 21:12–17

Key Verse: Jesus entered the temple area and drove out all who were buying and selling there. He overturned the tables of the money changers and the benches of those selling doves. (Matthew 21:12)

If you read this lesson on **www.lifeofchristweb.com**, be sure to click on the highlighted words and follow the additional links.

People came to the temple at Passover to worship God, offer sacrifices, make offerings, and pay a yearly temple tax. They came from far away, so they would buy animals for the sacrifices near the temple. They also needed to change their local money for the kind of coins used in the temple. The court of the Gentiles was the outer area of the temple where people who weren't Jews could worship. Some people set up shop there, selling animals and exchanging money for high fees. They were taking advantage of the people who came to worship, making them pay more than was necessary. Their marketplace also took up space where outsiders were supposed to be able to pray. Jesus didn't like it one bit!

Jesus went into the temple area. He chased out all the people who were buying and selling where they should have been worshiping God and praying. He turned over their tables. Mark's gospel says some people were walking through the temple carrying things to sell. They may have been using the temple as a shortcut to get to the marketplace. Jesus stopped them. As he was chasing the money-changers out, he said, "It is written, 'My house will be called a house of prayer,' but you are making it a 'den for robbers.'"

Those who were misusing God's temple ran away. But some people ran to Jesus. Blind and sick people came to Jesus. And he healed them. The children also ran to Jesus. They praised him, shouting, "Hosanna to the Son of David!" When the chief priests and teachers of the law heard this, they became angry. "Son of David" was a name for the Messiah. They asked Jesus if he heard what the children were saying. He heard! And he knew the children were doing what God's Word said they would do. Jesus replied to the chief priests and teachers of the law, "... have you never read, 'From the lips of children and infants you have ordained praise.'" That was a quote from Psalm 8:2, saying that children and infants would praise the Lord. Jesus is the Lord!

After that, Jesus left the temple and went out to the city of Bethany. He spent the night there. Bethany is the city where Lazarus, Mary, and Martha lived.

Discussion Questions **Name** ______________________________

- What was wrong with the actions of the merchants in the court of the Gentiles?

- Why did Jesus take such strong action?

- Why did the children respond to Jesus this way?

- What does this lesson tell us about Jesus' priorities for his people?

- What questions do you have about Jesus, and why are those questions important to you?

Lesson 30 Review Quiz: Disruption at the Temple

1. Why did people need money and animals at the temple?

They needed the type of coins used in the temple, and the animals for sacrifices.

They needed to pay to take the temple tour.

They needed money to buy food and animals to ride on.

They needed money to pay to have their animals groomed.

2. Name the part of the temple in which people who were not Jews worshiped.

The church of the pagans

The court of the Gentiles

The Most Holy Place

The room of the Ark

3. What did Jesus say was wrong at the temple that day?

People were making God's house into a den for robbers.

It was so crowded that people could not see him.

The priests were doing the sacrifices wrong.

Children kept shouting when they should have been quiet.

4. What unusual thing did Jesus do at the temple that day?

He taught the people about the Law.

He yelled at the priests and beat them with a rod.

He chased out the people misusing God's temple and turned over their tables.

He let all the animals out of their cages so they wouldn't be sacrificed.

5. What did the children shout at Jesus?

Hosanna to the Son of David!

Crucify him! Crucify him!

Hey, don't forget the little ones!

Who are you?

6. Where did Jesus go to spend the night after he left the temple?

Nazareth, where he grew up

A stable in Bethlehem

A hotel

Bethany, where Lazarus, Martha, and Mary lived

Lesson 31: **New Meaning to the Passover Meal**

Topic: Remembering Jesus' death and its meaning

Scripture: Luke 22:14–23

Key Verse: And he [Jesus] took bread, gave thanks and broke it, and gave it to them [the apostles], saying, "This is my body given for you; do this in remembrance of me." In the same way, after the supper he took the cup, saying, "This cup is the new covenant in my blood, which is poured out for you." (Luke 22:19–20)

If you read this lesson on **www.lifeofchristweb.com**, be sure to click on the highlighted words and follow the additional links.

Jews celebrate Passover every year to remember when God freed them from slavery in Egypt. Back in Egypt they had to kill a lamb and put its blood on the doorposts of their homes, so the angel of death would pass over them. That protected them from God's curse. God told the Jews to have a special meal at a special time each year to remember what God had done to free them. Important parts of the meal were these: a sacrificial lamb, unleavened bread, and the cup of wine. Jesus was about to give new meaning to the Passover meal.

Jesus ate his last Passover meal with his disciples the night before he died on the cross. This meal is sometimes called the Last Supper. During this meal, Jesus told the disciples that one of them would betray him. That was Judas. Judas left before the meal was over. Jesus said he wouldn't eat the Passover again until he ate it with them in his Father's kingdom. Then Jesus served the cup and the bread. He told his followers to remember his death, and its meaning, by taking the cup and the bread until he comes back. This is called communion.

Jesus gave new meaning to the Passover meal. The main dish was lamb—a lamb that had been sacrificed. At the first Passover a lamb's blood protected them from God's curse of death. Jesus came to die on Passover. He is the lamb, sacrificed to pay for our sins. If we believe Jesus is our sacrifice, we are protected from God's judgment for our sins. We are protected from death.

The unleavened bread was a symbol of having no sin. Leaven is yeast that makes bread rise into a fluffy loaf. The Bible uses leaven as a symbol of evil or sin. Unleavened bread has no leaven. It's like a cracker and a symbol of having no sin. Jesus broke the unleavened bread and said, "This is my body. It is given for you." Jesus had no sin in him. He gave his sinless body for us.

After supper Jesus told them the cup of wine is the new covenant in his blood. A covenant is an agreement. The old agreement between God and people said that sin would be covered by the blood of sacrificed animals—every year. The new agreement said that Jesus' blood would be poured out as a sacrifice for sin. Jesus' blood is better than the blood of animals. His sacrifice is good forever.

Discussion Questions **Name** ______________________________

- Why was the Passover celebration significant for Jesus and his disciples?

- How was the Last Supper linked with Passover?

- How was the Last Supper different from the Passover meal?

- Why do Christians celebrate communion today?

- What questions do you have about Jesus, and why are those questions important to you?

Lesson 31 Review Quiz: New Meaning to the Passover Meal

1. What does the Passover feast celebrate?

The birth of Jesus

The time when God freed the Jews from slavery in Egypt

The time when Jesus rose from the dead and passed over Jerusalem

Passing over the Jordan River on dry ground

2. What were important parts of the Passover meal?

A sacrificial lamb, unleavened bread, and a cup of wine

Bread and water

An item from each of the five Jewish food groups

Fresh fruit and fish

3. What happened at the Last Supper?

Judas complained about the food.

Jesus was arrested.

Jesus appeared to his disciples and disappeared.

Jesus told his disciples that one of them would betray him.

4. What sacrificial animal did Jesus represent?

Dove

Donkey

Lamb

Camel

5. What does leaven (yeast that makes bread rise) represent in the Bible?

Sin or evil

Jesus' rising from the dead

Health

Goodness

6. What is the new covenant?

A book of the Bible

A Jewish holiday

A new agreement with your parents

A new agreement with God

Lesson 32: **Arrested, Tried and Tortured**

Topic: Jesus submits to his Father's will and undergoes great suffering

Scripture: Luke 22:47–23:25

Key Verse: Then seizing him [Jesus], they led him away and took him into the house of the high priest. Peter followed at a distance. (Luke 22:54)

If you read this lesson on **www.lifeofchristweb.com**, be sure to click on the highlighted words and follow the additional links.

After the Last Supper, Jesus and his disciples went to the Mount of Olives. He often prayed there. This night Jesus was very sad and troubled. He knew what was about to happen to him. He prayed three times, asking his Father in heaven to keep him from suffering—if there was any other way. He said, "Father, if you are willing, take this cup from me; yet not my will, but yours be done." He was in such agony that an angel came to him to give him strength.

A crowd came toward Jesus. Judas was leading the chief priests, the temple guard, and the elders. They were carrying clubs and swords. Judas kissed Jesus. That was the sign he said he would give. Peter was ready to fight for Jesus. He drew his sword and cut off the ear of one of the servants of the high priest. Jesus told him to put his sword away. Then he healed the man's ear.

First Jesus was taken to the house of the high priest. Peter followed along. Earlier, Jesus had told Peter that he would act like he didn't know him. Jesus said Peter would deny knowing him three times before the rooster crowed the next morning. Peter found that hard to believe. While Peter was waiting to see what would happen, people asked if he had been with Jesus. Three times Peter said he didn't even know Jesus. Then the rooster crowed. Jesus turned and looked right at Peter. Then Peter ran outside and sobbed.

The soldiers started making fun of Jesus and beating him. They blindfolded him and took turns slugging him. Then they said, "Prophesy! Who hit you?" At dawn the chief priests and teachers of the law held a trial. When Jesus admitted that he was the Son of God, they said he was guilty of blasphemy. They decided he should be put to death. But they had to get the Roman governor to pass the death sentence. So they took him to Pilate. Pilate had the authority to sentence Jesus to death, but he said, "I find no basis for a charge against this man." When he heard Jesus was from Galilee, he sent him to Herod. Herod was the governor over Galilee. And he was in Jerusalem for Passover. Herod asked Jesus many questions. But Jesus wouldn't answer him. The soldiers made fun of Jesus, dressed him up like a king, and put a crown of thorns on his head. But Herod found him "not guilty" of any crime that deserved death. So he sent him back to Pilate. Pilate tried to let him go. He, too, said Jesus had done nothing worthy of death. He wanted to whip him and let him go. But the crowd kept screaming, "Crucify him! Crucify him!" So Pilate did what they wanted. He ordered that Jesus be whipped and then crucified.

Discussion Questions **Name** ____________________________

- What does Jesus' prayer tell us about what he was going through?

- How did Judas' actions add to Jesus' suffering?

- Why do you think Peter denied knowing Jesus?
  What do you think was going through his mind?

- Why do you think the religious leaders refused to accept the not-guilty verdicts?

- What questions do you have about Jesus, and why are those questions important to you?

Lesson 32 Review Quiz: Arrested, Tried, and Tortured

1. Why did Jesus go to the Mount of Olives after the Last Supper?

He was trying to run away.

He went there to pray.

He went there to pick olives.

He went there to sleep.

2. What sign did Judas use to identify Jesus?

He kissed him.

He pointed at him.

He hugged him.

He made a mark on his robe.

3. What did Jesus tell Peter he would do three times before the rooster crowed?

Pray

Say he did not know Jesus

Cry

Eat bread with leaven in it

4. What did the chief priests and teachers of the law say Jesus was guilty of?

Murder

Blasphemy—claiming to be the Son of God

Riding a donkey on the Sabbath

Stealing

5. What did Herod's soldiers do to Jesus?

Arrested him.

Made fun of him, dressed him like a king and put a crown of thorns on his head.

Prayed for him.

Ran away from him.

6. When Pilate offered to let Jesus go, what did the crowd shout?

Blessed is he who comes in the name of the Lord!

Hosanna! Hosanna! Glory to God in the highest!

Hooray! Hooray!

Crucify him! Crucify him!

Lesson 33: **Jesus Goes to the Cross to Die for Us**

Topic: The penalty for our sin is paid in full

Scripture: Luke 23:26–49

Key Verse: When they came to the place called the Skull, there they crucified him [Jesus], along with the criminals—one on his right, the other on his left. Jesus said, "Father, forgive them, for they do not know what they are doing." (Luke 23:33–34a)

If you read this lesson on **www.lifeofchristweb.com**, be sure to click on the highlighted words and follow the additional links.

Jesus had been whipped terribly. Then he was forced to carry his wooden cross. A man named Simon carried the cross part of the way for Jesus. Many people followed. Some women cried loudly because their hearts were filled with sorrow. Jesus and two criminals were taken to a place called The Skull. Another word for "skull" in Latin is Calvaria. That's why people now say Jesus died at Calvary. There they nailed Jesus to the cross to die.

As Jesus was being crucified, he said, "Father, forgive them, for they do not know what they are doing." The soldiers divided up his clothes and gambled to see who would keep them. They didn't realize they were fulfilling words in Psalm 22:16 and 18. There it says, "A band of evil men has encircled me, they have pierced my hands and my feet… . People stare and gloat over me. They divide my garments among them and cast lots for my clothing." (See Psalm 22:16-18) All of that happened to Jesus.

The people stood there watching. The rulers even made fun of Jesus. They said, "He saved others; let him save himself if he is the Christ of God, the Chosen One." The soldiers mocked him. One of the criminals hanging beside Jesus insulted him, saying, "Aren't you the Christ? Save yourself and us!" He was mocking Jesus. The other criminal sincerely put his faith in Jesus. He said, "Jesus, remember me when you come into your kingdom." Jesus answered him, "I tell you the truth, today you will be with me in paradise."

A sign was placed above Jesus. It said, "THIS IS THE KING OF THE JEWS." At about noon the sun stopped shining. It was dark for about three hours while Jesus was dying. Matthew's gospel says that there was also an earthquake. A special curtain in the temple was torn from top to bottom. This curtain kept people out of the Most Holy Place—where the priest came into God's presence. God tore the curtain. This showed that the death of Jesus made it possible for people to go directly into God's presence. Then Jesus called out in a loud voice, "Father, into your hands I commit my spirit." Then Jesus died.

Many people watched Jesus die: his mother, his followers, the women from Galilee, and the crowds. The Roman commander saw all that happened when Jesus died. He said, "Surely this was a righteous man."

Discussion Questions Name ______________________________

- What made crucifixion such a horrible means of execution?

- How did people near Jesus' cross react to his crucifixion?

- How did Jesus respond to what was going on around him?

- What are some of the things that happened when Jesus died?

- Why is Jesus' death important for people today?

- What questions do you have about Jesus, and why are those questions important to you?

Lesson 33 Review Quiz: Jesus Goes to the Cross to Die for Us

1. What was Jesus forced to carry?

His cross

Simon's cross

A soldier's backpack

Large stones

2. Where was Jesus taken to be crucified?

The place of the cross

The place of the skull

The tower

Herod's palace

3. What did the soldiers do with Jesus' robe?

Burned it to keep themselves warm.

Gave it to his mother.

Ripped it to pieces, and each soldier kept a piece.

Gambled to see who would get it.

4. What did Jesus say to the thief who asked to be remembered in his kingdom?

Someday you will be with me in paradise.

You are not worthy. Criminals cannot be saved.

Today, you will be with me in paradise.

What kingdom? Can't you see that it's over!

5. What did the sign say that was placed over Jesus on the cross?

This man says he is King of the Jews.

Rome Rules!

Surrender!

This is the King of the Jews.

6. What did the Roman commander say about Jesus after he died?

What a brave man!

Jesus was surely a man who did what was right!

He saved others; too bad he couldn't save himself.

What a waste!

7 Jesus Is Alive Forever and Ever

Lesson 34: **The Burial and Resurrection**

Topic: The transformation from deep sorrow to overwhelming joy

Scripture: Matthew 27:57–28:15, Luke 24:1–7

Key Verse: The angel said to the women, "Do not be afraid, for I know that you are looking for Jesus, who was crucified. He is not here; he has risen, just as he said. Come and see the place where he lay." (Matthew 28:5–6)

If you read this lesson on **www.lifeofchristweb.com**, be sure to click on the highlighted words and follow the additional links.

A rich man named Joseph was a disciple of Jesus. He asked Pilate if he could bury Jesus' body. Pilate gave the order. Joseph carefully took the body of Jesus and wrapped it in clean linen cloth. Then he laid it in his own new tomb near where Jesus was crucified. The tomb was like a cave cut out of the rock. He rolled a giant stone in front of the entrance of the tomb and went away.

The chief priests and teachers of the law went to Pilate. They remembered that Jesus said he would rise from the dead on the third day. They were afraid the disciples would steal the body and say Jesus had risen from the dead. So Pilate sent a group of Roman soldiers to guard the tomb. They camped outside the tomb to make sure no one stole the body of Jesus.

Just as he promised, Jesus came back alive on the third day—and the soldiers were there as witnesses! An angel came down from heaven and there was a powerful earthquake. The angel rolled back the great stone and sat on it. He looked like lightning. His clothes were white as snow. The guards were so scared they shook with fright and fainted.

Mary Magdalene and other women went to the tomb at dawn on the first day of the week. They saw the angel, too. He told them, "Do not be afraid, for I know that you are looking for Jesus, who was crucified. He is not here; he has risen, just as he said." The angel invited them to see the empty tomb where Jesus had been lying. Then he said, "... go quickly and tell his disciples: 'He has risen from the dead and is going ahead of you into Galilee. There you will see him.'"

The women were afraid, but they were also filled with great joy. Suddenly Jesus met them and greeted them. They fell down, took hold of Jesus' feet, and worshiped him. He told them, "Do not be afraid. Go and tell my brothers to go to Galilee; there they will see me." The women ran to tell the disciples.

Meanwhile, the soldiers ran to tell the chief priests what had happened. When they told them, the chief priests and the elders had another emergency meeting. They decided to pay the soldiers to lie and say that the disciples stole Jesus' body. They also promised to make sure the soldiers didn't get in trouble with the governor. The soldiers agreed to tell that lie. Some people still believe it.

Discussion Questions **Name** ________________________________

- What things seem unusual to you about Jesus' burial?

- Why do you think God sent angels to the tomb?

- How did the soldiers react to the angels?
  How do you explain the reaction of the women?

- How did the women react when they encountered Jesus?

- Why is Jesus' resurrection important for people today?

- What questions do you have about Jesus, and why are those questions important to you?

Lesson 34 Review Quiz: The Burial and Resurrection

1. Name the man who asked Pilate for the body of Jesus.

Nicodemus

Joseph

Peter

John

2. Why did Pilate send Roman soldiers to guard Jesus' tomb?

He wanted to keep the curious people away.

The chief priests and teachers of the law feared someone would steal his body.

The guards wanted to see Jesus rise from the dead.

He didn't want anyone to be able to anoint Jesus' body with perfume.

3. What happened on the third day after Jesus' death?

Jesus went back to heaven.

Jesus woke up from a deep sleep.

Jesus rose from the dead in his resurrected body.

Jesus came back as a ghost.

4. What powerful event of nature happened at Jesus' tomb?

A tornado

An earthquake

Thunder and lightning

A mighty wind

5. What did the soldiers do when they saw the angel roll back the stone?

They ran around screaming.

They shook with fright and fainted.

They drew their swords and commanded the angel to come down off the stone.

They ran and hid in the garden until the angel disappeared.

6. How did the chief priests respond to the soldiers' news of what happened?

They had the soldiers sent to Pilate to be punished.

They cut out their tongues so that they couldn't tell anyone.

They paid the soldiers to lie and say the disciples came and stole Jesus' body.

They believed that Jesus was the true Messiah and became his followers.

Lesson 35: **The Resurrected Jesus Visits Friends and Followers**

Topic: Jesus encourages and instructs his bewildered, yet joyful followers.

Scripture: Luke 24:13–44

Key Verse: [Jesus] … appeared first to Mary Magdalene… . Afterward Jesus appeared in a different form to two of them while they were walking in the country… . Later Jesus appeared to the Eleven as they were eating. (Mark 16:9a, 12, 14a)

If you read this lesson on **www.lifeofchristweb.com**, be sure to click on the highlighted words and follow the additional links.

Mary Magdalene and the other women ran to tell the disciples that Jesus was alive. But the men didn't believe them. Meanwhile, two of Jesus' followers were walking to Emmaus, a village about seven miles from Jerusalem. They were very sad. They were talking about all that had happened in the last few days. Jesus came up and started walking with them, but they could not recognize him.

Jesus asked them what they were talking about. They told him how they HAD hoped that Jesus was the Messiah. But the chief priests handed him over to be crucified. They no longer called Jesus Messiah; now they called him a prophet. Then they told Jesus how some women had seen angels who said Jesus was alive. They told him how some of the disciples had found the tomb empty—just like the women said. But they were still sad and confused.

Jesus said to them, "How foolish you are, and how slow of heart to believe all that the prophets have spoken! Did not the Christ have to suffer these things and then enter his glory?" Jesus explained to them what was said about himself in all the Scriptures. He began with Moses and all the prophets. They still didn't know it was Jesus! When they got to where they were staying, they urged him to stay with them because it was getting late. When Jesus was at the table with them, getting ready to eat, he gave thanks, broke the bread, and began to give it to them. Then their eyes were opened so they could recognize Jesus. As soon as they did, He disappeared!

The two men returned to Jerusalem as fast as they could and joined the disciples who were gathered there. They told them how Jesus had walked with them and how he disappeared when they recognized him. Can you imagine how excited they must have been! While they were still talking, Jesus suddenly appeared! He was right there with them! They thought he was a ghost, so Jesus let them touch his body—which a ghost doesn't have. He showed them the wounds where the nails went through his hands and feet. He even ate food to prove he was really risen from the dead—not just a spirit. Then Jesus said, "This is what I told you while I was still with you: Everything must be fulfilled that is written about me in the Law of Moses, the Prophets, and the Psalms." Then Jesus opened their minds to understand. And they did.

Discussion Questions **Name** ____________________________

- Why do you think some disciples had trouble believing that Jesus was alive?

- How would you describe the feelings of the two disciples before Jesus joined them?

- What parts of the Old Testament do you think Jesus mentioned?

- How would you describe feelings of the two disciples after Jesus revealed himself to them?

- Why do you think Jesus allowed the disciples to touch him and see him eat?

- What questions do you have about Jesus, and why are those questions important to you?

Lesson 35 Review Quiz: The Resurrected Jesus Visits Friends and Followers

1. How did the apostles react when the women said Jesus was alive?

They didn't believe it.

They praised God and remembered the prophecies.

They immediately headed for Galilee to meet the Lord, as he told them to do.

They were angry that the women would make up such a story.

2. Name the village seven miles from Jerusalem where the two disciples were going.

Bethany

Capernaum

Mary's village

Emmaus

3. What were the two disciples discussing as they left Jerusalem?

What they were going to do with their lives now that Jesus was dead.

How bravely Jesus died.

The events of the past few days (Jesus' crucifixion, reports of the empty tomb).

How much their feet hurt from walking so far.

4. What did Jesus say to the two disciples (before they knew it was Jesus)?

Don't be discouraged. You'll find something to do with your lives.

He explained all that Moses and the prophets had written about the Messiah.

Jesus was a good man, and a good prophet, but he wasn't the Messiah.

He told them when God would set up his kingdom on earth.

5. At what point did the two men realize the "stranger" was really Jesus?

When they noticed the wounds in his hands and feet.

When Jesus washed their feet before dinner.

When Jesus changed his clothes.

When Jesus gave thanks and broke the bread at dinner.

6. What did Jesus do when he appeared to the apostles in Jerusalem?

Asked why they hadn't gone to Galilee, where the women told them to meet him.

Scolded them for running away when he got arrested.

Showed them his wounds and ate with them to prove he was not a ghost.

Told them how painful it was to be crucified.

Lesson 36: **Saying Good-Bye and Spreading Good News**

Topic: Jesus leaves and the Father sends the Holy Spirit to comfort, guide, and empower the believers.

Scripture: Matthew 28:18–20, Luke 24:45–48, Acts 1:1–9

Key Verse: "But you will receive power when the Holy Spirit comes on you; and you will be my witnesses in Jerusalem, and in all Judea and Samaria, and to the ends of the earth." After he [Jesus] said this, he was taken up before their very eyes, and a cloud hid him from their sight. (Acts 1: 8–9)

If you read this lesson on **www.lifeofchristweb.com**, be sure to click on the highlighted words and follow the additional links.

Jesus continued to appear to his disciples for forty days after he rose from the dead. He spoke to them about the kingdom of God. He explained how he had to suffer and rise from the dead on the third day to fulfill the prophecies. He told them they were witnesses of these things. They thought Jesus was going to set up his kingdom on earth right then. Jesus said it was not for them to know when God would bring the kingdom to earth. Their job was to spread the good news.

One day Jesus was eating with them. He gave them a command. "Do not leave Jerusalem, but wait for the gift my Father promised, which you have heard me speak about. For John baptized with water, but in a few days you will be baptized with the Holy Spirit." The prophet Joel said that God would pour out his Spirit on all who serve Him. The disciples would need God's Holy Spirit and God's power to do what God planned for them to do.

Jesus told his disciples to preach about all he had done and to tell people to turn from their sins and receive God's forgiveness. He told them to start in Jerusalem, spread to the surrounding areas of Judea and Samaria, then go to the whole world. Jesus said, "All authority in heaven and on earth has been given to me. Therefore go and make disciples of all nations, baptizing them in the name of the Father and of the Son and of the Holy Spirit, and teaching them to obey everything I have commanded you. And surely I am with you always, to the very end of the age." This command is often called the Great Commission. Before Jesus died, they just preached to the Jews, now they would preach to everyone.

Forty days after his resurrection, Jesus was on the Mount of Olives with his followers. He lifted up his hands and blessed them. While he was blessing them, he began to float up into the air. They watched him go. They didn't take their eyes off him until the clouds covered him and they couldn't see him anymore. Suddenly, two men dressed in white stood with them. This is how angels often appeared. "Men of Galilee" they said, "why do you stand here looking into the sky? This same Jesus, who has been taken from you into heaven, will come back in the same way you have seen him go into heaven." So they worshiped him and returned to Jerusalem filled with great joy. They waited there until they were filled with the Holy Spirit and received power from heaven. Then they spent the rest of their lives spreading the good news about Jesus and making disciples all over the world.

Discussion Questions **Name** ________________________________

- What was Jesus doing between his resurrection and his ascension into heaven?

- Why did Jesus tell his disciples to stay in Jerusalem for a while?

- What is the Great Commission? Why is it still important today?

- What do you think was significant about Jesus' ascension?

- How can we know what Jesus wants us to do?

- What questions do you have about Jesus, and why are those questions important to you?

Lesson 36 Review Quiz: Saying Good-bye and Spreading Good News

1. How many days did Jesus stay on earth after he rose from the dead?

Four days

Forty days

Four weeks

Four months

2. Jesus told the disciples it was their job ...

to collect money in the temple.

to spread the good news.

to overthrow the Roman government.

to tell stories about how Pilate treated him.

3. Why did Jesus tell the disciples to wait in Jerusalem?

Because it was the safest place for them.

To wait for the gift his Father promised, being baptized with the Holy Spirit.

To see what would happen to the chief priests and teachers of the law.

To set up his kingdom on earth in Jerusalem.

4. Why did they need to receive this gift before they left Jerusalem?

To receive God's power to be able to do what God planned for them to do.

So they could walk on water.

So they could show all their friends.

So the chief priests and teachers of the law would finally believe in Jesus.

5. What's the name for the command Jesus gave them to go and make disciples?

The Great Story

The Great Adventure

The Great Commission

The Great Commandment

6. What happened as Jesus was blessing his disciples on the Mount of Olives?

He gave the Sermon on the Mount.

He floated up into the air until the clouds covered him.

The chief priests and soldiers came and arrested him again.

The disciples finally recognized he was Jesus.

Lesson 37: **Jesus Selects Another Apostle**

Topic: The conversion and calling of the apostle Paul

Scripture: Acts 8:1–4, Acts 9:1–31

Key Verse: But the Lord said to Ananias, "Go! This man is my chosen instrument to carry my name before the Gentiles and their kings and before the people of Israel." (Acts 9:15)

If you read this lesson on **www.lifeofchristweb.com**, be sure to click on the highlighted words and follow the additional links.

Jesus' disciples waited in Jerusalem like Jesus told them. On the day of Pentecost they were all together. A sound like a mighty wind filled the room. Tongues of fire appeared over each one and they were baptized with the Holy Spirit. Then they began to spread the good news, starting in Jerusalem. The Jewish leaders who called for Jesus' death fought against them. They even killed one of his followers named Stephen, by stoning him. A Jewish leader named Saul guarded the clothes of those who killed Stephen. He fully approved of what they did.

Saul was raised in the Jewish religion. He was taught by Gamaliel, one of the best Jewish teachers of the law. Saul believed that Jesus was a false prophet. He thought all of Jesus' followers deserved to die. Saul decided to do everything he could to stop them from spreading what he thought were lies. Saul went house to house searching for Jesus' followers. If he found them, he dragged them off and threw them in prison. He kept threatening to kill the Lord's disciples. The news of Jesus was spreading. Saul determined to stop it. He got letters from the high priest saying he could arrest anyone who followed Jesus. Then he headed for Damascus, a large city about 150 miles from Jerusalem. He planned to arrest everyone he found who followed Jesus. Suddenly a light from heaven flashed around him. He fell to the ground. He heard a voice speak to him. "Saul, Saul, why do you persecute me?" "Who are you, Lord?" Saul asked. "I am Jesus, whom you are persecuting," he replied. "Now get up and go into the city, and you will be told what you must do." (Acts 9:3-6) When Saul got up, he was blind. He was led into the city. For three days he didn't eat or drink.

Meanwhile, Jesus spoke to a man named Ananias in a vision. He told him what happened and told him where to find Saul. He told Ananias to go pray for Saul to receive his sight and receive the Holy Spirit. Ananias was afraid. He had heard about Saul. "But the Lord said to Ananias, 'Go! This man is my chosen instrument to carry my name before the Gentiles and their kings and before the people of Israel.'" Jesus used Saul powerfully! You may know him by his other name, the apostle Paul. Paul went on three missionary journeys, creating churches all over the world. He preached the good news before kings. He also wrote more books of the New Testament than any other writer. Finally, he was put in prison and killed for his faith in Jesus.

Discussion Questions **Name** ________________________________

- Why were the events on Pentecost important to Jesus' disciples?

- Why was there so much animosity toward Jesus' followers?
  What was Saul's motivation for persecuting Christians?

- How did Jesus call Saul?

- What do you think Ananias felt when he received the vision?

- What can we learn from the fact that Jesus called Saul?

- What questions do you have about Jesus, and why are those questions important to you?

Lesson 37 Review Quiz: Jesus Selects Another Apostle

1. *What was the name of the disciple stoned to death while Saul watched?*

Stephen

Matthew

Mark

Saul

2. *Saul believed that Jesus was a(n) ____________________.*

bad man

false prophet

good man

angel

3. *Saul went from house to house, doing what to Jesus' followers?*

Inviting them to dinner.

Trying to make them reject Jesus.

Dragging them out and throwing them into prison.

Honoring them.

4. *Who appeared to Saul and spoke to him on the road to Damascus?*

Robbers

Elijah and Moses

Jesus

Paul and Silas

5. *By what other name do most people know the man called Saul in this story?*

Apostle Peter

Apostle Paul

Apostle John

Saul the Great

6. *What did Saul do for the rest of his life?*

Tried to stop people from believing in Jesus.

Served Jesus, went on three missionary journeys, and wrote 13 books of the Bible.

Made tents and retired in Joppa.

Married and had twelve sons.

Lesson 38: **The Devil's Destruction**

Topic: God's victory over Satan is complete

Scripture: Ephesians 6:10–18; Revelation 20:10

Key Verse: The devil has been sinning from the beginning. The reason the Son of God appeared was to destroy the devil's work. (1 John 3:8b)

If you read this lesson on **www.lifeofchristweb.com**, be sure to click on the highlighted words and follow the additional links.

Jesus came to save us from our sins. But our sins didn't come from nowhere. Sin started way back in the Garden of Eden. The first two people God created, Adam and Eve, were tempted to disobey God. The one who tempted them is the evil one. Sometimes he is described as a snake, a dragon, the devil, or Satan. The Bible tells us that the evil one used to be an angel named Lucifer, but he tried to put himself higher than God. He was thrown out of heaven. Since then he came to earth to fight against God and try to destroy the people God loves.

While Jesus was on earth, he fought against the devil. The devil fooled people into believing lies. Jesus brought the truth. The devil caused people to be blind spiritually—unable to see God's way. Jesus made blind people see; he opened their eyes and their minds to see the truth. The devil tormented some people. His demons, other evil spirits who followed the devil, took over their minds and bodies, throwing them into fire or causing them to hurt themselves. Jesus commanded these evil spirits to get out of people. Only then were these people free from torment. They were back in control of their bodies and in their right mind. The devil caused disease and pain. Jesus healed people who were sick. The devil led people away from God. Jesus led people to God. Jesus called the devil a thief who comes to kill and steal and destroy. Jesus came to give people life in the fullest possible way. Jesus came to destroy the works of the devil.

The devil is still at work on the earth today. That's why there is so much sin, sorrow, suffering, violence, sickness, and death. Jesus promised his followers the help they would need to overcome all the power of the evil one. But Christians must fight against the forces of evil. The Holy Spirit came to lead those who love Jesus into truth. The armor of God is given to protect us from the devil's attacks. Jesus taught us to pray that God will keep us from falling into sin when the evil one tempts us. We have God's help, but there is still a battle going on. One day that battle will be over. Jesus will get rid of the devil forever!

Many years after Jesus went back to heaven, the apostle John was arrested for spreading the good news. He was sent to the Island of Patmos so he couldn't tell more people about Jesus. While John was there, the Lord showed him a vision of Jesus and what would happen at the end of the world. This vision showed him what Jesus would finally do with the devil. He will throw the devil into a lake of fire, burning with sulfur. He will never be able to escape to hurt or fool anyone ever again. The devil will suffer "day and night forever and ever."

Discussion Questions

Name ______________________________

- Why is it important for us to be aware of Satan and his work?

- In the Gospels, how did Jesus fight against Satan's power?

- How powerful is Satan today?
  What are some ways he tries to influence people's behavior?

- How does the Holy Spirit enable us to counteract Satan's work?

- Why have so many Christians found the book of Revelation so encouraging?

- What questions do you have about Jesus, and why are those questions important to you?

Lesson 38 Review Quiz: The Devil's Destruction

1. Name the first people who sinned and where it happened.

The people of Israel at the foot of Mount Sinai

Samson and Delilah in the land of the Philistines

Adam and Eve in the Garden of Eden

Lot and his family at Sodom and Gomorrah

2. Who was Jesus really fighting against while he was on earth?

Murderers, liars, thieves, cheaters, sinners, and haters of God

The chief priests and teachers of the law

The devil and all spiritual forces of evil

All unbelievers

3. Why is there sin, sorrow, suffering, violence, sickness, and death on earth?

Because the devil is still at work on earth today

Because people are so bad

Because God doesn't love people

Because people see it on TV and do what they see

4. What does God give us to protect us from the attacks of the devil?

The armor of God

The holy shield

A magic book

Books to make us happy and forget about Satan

5. Who wrote down what God says will happen to the devil?

The apostle Paul

The apostle John

The apostle Peter

Mary, the mother of Jesus

6. What will God finally do to destroy the works of the devil?

Throw him into a lake of fire, where he will suffer forever and ever.

Put him in chains.

Put him in prison.

Make him promise to be good.

Lesson 39: **God Makes All Things New**

Topic: The anticipation of a new heaven and a new earth

Scripture: Revelation 21:1–22:6

Key Verse: Then I saw a new heaven and a new earth, for the first heaven and the first earth had passed away, and there was no longer any sea. (Revelation 21:1)

If you read this lesson on **www.lifeofchristweb.com**, be sure to click on the highlighted words and follow the additional links.

People worry about where they will go when they die. Jesus told his followers not to let their hearts be troubled. He said that his Father's house has many wonderful places in which to live. Jesus said he was going away to prepare a place for all who love him. He promised to come back and take his followers to that special place so they all can live with him forever.

Most people say they want to go to heaven. But heaven will be greater than anything we can imagine. 1 Corinthians 2:9 says, "No eye has seen, no ear has heard, no mind has conceived what God has prepared for those who love him." It will be awesome.

The book of Revelation describes what God will do to make a special place for those who love him. It's a whole new heaven and a whole new earth. God created a beautiful earth for us to enjoy: mountains, oceans, flowers, and beautiful scenery. But this earth has been damaged. It was cursed when Adam and Eve sinned. When God's will is finally done on earth, there will no longer be any curse. God is going to make a brand new earth where everything is perfect!

Revelation also describes a new Jerusalem from which God will rule. The city of Jerusalem on earth today is beautiful, but nothing like the new Jerusalem. The new Jerusalem will have streets paved with gold. It will have walls made of gold and filled with jewels.

The old city of Jerusalem had a great temple. The new Jerusalem will have God himself! And God's people will see his face. There will be no more night. They will not need the light of a lamp or the light of the sun. The Lord God will give them light. Those who love God will rule forever and ever. Revelation 22:27b says that only those whose names are written in the Lamb's Book of Life will enter the city.

The disciple John heard a loud voice from the throne saying, "'Now the dwelling of God is with men, and he will live with them. They will be his people, and God himself will be with them and be their God. He will wipe away every tear from their eyes. There will be no more death or mourning or crying or pain, for the old order of things has passed away.' He who was seated on the throne said, 'I am making everything new!' Then he said, 'Write this down, for these words are trustworthy and true.'" (Revelation 21:3–5)

Discussion Questions **Name** ______________________________

- How did the sin of Adam and Eve affect other created things?

- What attracts you most about heaven?

- What are some things that make the New Jerusalem so special?

- Why have so many Christians found the book of Revelation so encouraging?

- What questions do you have about Jesus, and why are those questions important to you?

Lesson 39 Review Quiz : God Makes All Things New

1. What did Jesus say he was going away to do?

To see what was going on in heaven.

To visit the other planets in our solar system.

To prepare a place for all who love him.

To relax after his hard time on earth.

2. Who has seen and heard what God has prepared for those who love him?

No one

Good people

People with a great imagination

People who have good eyes and ears

3. Revelation says God will make a new _________ and a new _________.

a new heaven and a new earth

a new ocean and a new desert

a new sun and a new moon

a new friend and a new enemy

4. When God's will is done, what will happen to the curse that's on the earth?

There will be no more curse.

The curse won't be quite so bad.

The curse will get worse.

The curse will only be on bad people.

5. Old Jerusalem had a temple. What will the new Jerusalem have instead?

God himself, living with his people

A synagogue

A greater temple

A church

6. When God's will is finally done, the Bible says there will be no more ...

excuses.

death, sadness, crying, or pain.

homework.

earth.

Lesson 40: **The Teachings of Jesus**

Topic: Receiving, understanding, and following Christ's commands and teachings

Scripture: Matthew chapters 5–7

Key Verse: Therefore go and make disciples of all nations. . . . teaching them to obey everything I have commanded you. (Matthew 28:19a, 20a)

If you read this lesson on **www.lifeofchristweb.com**, be sure to click on the highlighted words and follow the additional links.

You've heard about the awesome things Jesus did. Jesus also came to teach. Jesus was called Rabbi, which means teacher. To really know Jesus, you must also know his teachings. He told his disciples to go make more disciples, "teaching them to obey everything I have commanded you." If you want to be a disciple of Jesus, you must learn what he taught. Jesus made a great promise to those who learn what he taught. It says: "If you remain in me and my words remain in you, ask whatever you wish, and it will be given you." (John 15:7) That's a good reason to get Jesus' words into your heart and mind.

One of Jesus' most famous sermons is called The Sermon on the Mount (he gave it on a mountainside). In that sermon Jesus taught how to be blessed. He explained how God expects people to live. Jesus taught that it's not just what we do that matters, but what is in our hearts. He seemed to make the Old Testament law more difficult. People had heard they should love their neighbor, but Jesus told them to love their enemies too. Jesus made it clear that no one can live the way God wants without his help.

Jesus taught people what God's kingdom is like. He taught how to pray and how to forgive. He taught that God's whole law comes down to two rules: 1) Love God with all your heart, soul, mind, and strength. 2) Love others as you love yourself. Jesus used stories called parables. These stories used examples from everyday life to teach spiritual truth. These parables were like riddles. Some people didn't get the point. Sometimes even the disciples didn't get the point. Then Jesus would explain what the parable meant so the disciples could understand. Jesus taught in parables to make the meaning clear to those who loved God and to keep it hidden from those who did not love God.

Everything Jesus taught agreed with God's word in the Old Testament. When he was only twelve, Jesus knew God's word. He amazed the teachers at the temple in Jerusalem. He asked them good questions and showed that he was wise with godly wisdom. You too can get to know God's word, even though you are young. You can ask good questions. You can become wise by learning the teachings of Jesus. The word "disciple" actually means "learner." If you want to be a disciple of Jesus, learn what he taught. God hid his truth from men who prided themselves on being wise, but showed his truth to all who opened their hearts to learn from him—even young people. God can show his truth to you too. Jesus is the truth. His teachings will show you the truth.

Discussion Questions **Name** ______________________________

- As you think back on all you've learned about Jesus in this course, what events in Jesus' life are most memorable?

- What words of Jesus are especially meaningful to you?

- If someone were to ask you why it's important to know who Jesus is, how would you answer?

- What questions do you have about Jesus, and why are those questions important to you?

- What are some specific things you can do to learn more about Jesus and follow him?

Lesson 40 Review Quiz: The Teachings of Jesus

1. What does the word "rabbi" mean?

Great leader

God with us

Messiah

Teacher

2. What did Jesus tell his disciples to teach others?

Teach them how to fish on the Sea of Galilee.

Teach them to obey everything I have commanded you.

Teach them to chase money-changers out of the temple.

Teach them how to get the Pharisees really angry.

3. What promise did Jesus make to those who remain in him and learn his words?

The world will never be destroyed by a flood again.

They will not have to pay taxes.

They will have as many children as there are stars in the heavens.

Ask whatever you wish, and it will be done for you.

4. What is the name of one of Jesus' most famous sermons?

The Sermon on the Mount

The story of David and Goliath

The Sermon by the Sea

The Salt of the Earth

5. What is the name of the stories Jesus told using examples from life?

Fairy tales

Parables

Legends

Sermons

6. What does the word "disciple" mean?

Fisherman

Learner

Apostle

Leader